TORQUAY UNITED

The first 70 Years

Laura Joint

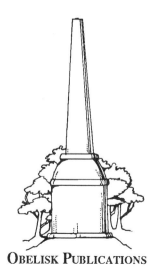

OBELISK PUBLICATIONS

The author:
Laura Joint is a news journalist and the Torquay United correspondent on the *Western Morning News*. Born and bred in Torquay, she has followed the Gulls, at home and away, since the 1960s.

Acknowledgements:
Pictures supplied by Colin Bratcher, Paul Levie, Andy Smurthwaite, Leigh Edwards, Devon and Exeter Press, Western Morning News, Alan Grinsill at Torquay United Social Club, and Manchester United FC. Thanks also to the following for help with statistics and facts from years well beyond my memory: John Lovis, Leigh Edwards and Basil Easterbrook. Additional thanks to everyone who has helped me, including Tony Jordan, for letting me use snippets from the Torquay United fanzine *Mission Impossible*.

This book is dedicated to Mum, Dad, Duncan and Lesley

First published in 1991
by Obelisk Publications
2 Church Hill, Pinhoe, Exeter, Devon
Designed and typeset by Chips & Sally Barber
Printed in Great Britain by
Penwell Ltd., Callington, Cornwall

CONTENTS

Torquay United FC

FOREWORD BY FRANK O'FARRELL

Through all my travels during my managerial career, which has taken me as far afield as Manchester United and the Middle East, Torquay United has always held an affectionate place in my heart. It was the club which gave me my first break in league management in 1965, when the Chairman, Tony Boyce, approached me and asked if I would like to become the manager. I spent three happy years at Plainmoor between 1965 and 1968, during which time I was able to bring many First Division players down to Torquay because they were so impressed by the progressive way in which the club was

run. I was also happy to help out the club in its hour of need on two further occasions in the late 1970s and the early 1980s. Although only a small club, and in an area not steeped in football tradition, it is an integral part of the town and, as attendances during the 1960s showed, Torquay United has several thousand loyal, if at times suffering, supporters. The last twenty five years have brought with them a whole series of ups and downs at Plainmoor. First, under myself, we were promoted to the Third Division. We very nearly achieved promotion to Division Two in 1968, but narrowly failed. Then, in 1972, United were relegated to Division Four where, unfortunately, they have remained ever since. The club only survived in the Football League in 1987 on goal difference, but bounced back to nearly win promotion the following year — and in 1989, they reached a Wembley cup final ... football certainly is a funny old game. Through all the turbulence, Torquay United has reached its seventieth year as a professional football club. I am pleased to have played a part in a successful chapter in the club's history, and hope there are many similarly successful chapters ahead.

4

1. THE EARLY YEARS

There have been times, as any Torquay United supporter will readily testify, when following the fortunes of the Gulls could best be described as an exercise in masochism. But the good times and a never-to-be-forgotten Wembley final have more than made up for the traumatic times which saw the club only survive in the Football League by the skin of a police dog's teeth just four seasons ago. Yet survive they did, and this season marks the club's seventieth year as a professional outfit.

It was back in 1921 that Torquay United was born — or perhaps that should be reborn, for Torquay United had actually kicked off in 1899. They joined with Ellacombe Football Club in 1910 and became known as Torquay Town, which then amalgamated with Babbacombe FC. Having previously played their football at Teignmouth Road, Torquay Recreation Ground and Barton Road, the club then took residence at their present Plainmoor ground in 1910. Finally, in 1921, the club went professional and reverted back to its original name. There has been a certain amount of argument over exactly when Torquay United was re-formed, with some literature referring to the momentous occasion not actually taking place until 1922. The club itself, however, along with United historians, state that 1921 was indeed the year that Torquay United started in earnest.

The man behind the club shedding its amateur days was Mr Charles Dear, who became the first honorary secretary of Torquay United. United played that first year of 1921/22 in the Western League, before joining the Southern League a year later where they played the likes of Boscombe, Bath City, Plymouth Argyle Reserves, Exeter City Reserves and Aberavon Athletic. They gave a good account of themselves in the early years, finishing sixth and fourth in their first two seasons.

In fact, that sixth position earned in their first year in the Southern League prompted United to apply for entry into the Football League Division Three (South). But United did not receive a single vote from the league clubs at their AGM and Boscombe — now known as Bournemouth — were elected after finishing second in the Southern League.

It must be said that it was a rather cheeky application by United, and one which was not realistically expected to succeed.

After those promising early seasons, the 1924/25 year proved to be not such a great success and United ended up sixth from bottom of the twenty-club league.

The following year heralded the arrival of left-back Percy Mackrill, who was probably one of the club's first great players. The season was very nearly United's last as they were threatened with extinction just four years after they had turned professional. The great storms of the 1925 winter blew away the grandstand roof (not for the last time) and, lacking the money to repair it, the

Torquay United's regular line-up during the 1925/6 season — the year before they won the Southern League: (L to R) Back Row: Marlow, Hughes, Rice, Bayes, Garratt, Leslie, Chambers, Pratt (trainer); Front Row: Vallance, Bell, Mackrill (player-manager), Appleyard, Pither

club was in danger of having to close down. They were saved after the local public and their Devon footballing rivals came to the rescue.

Both Plymouth Argyle and Exeter City played United in fund-raising matches which, along with generous donations from the public, was enough to save the Plainmoor club from financial ruin.

It was well worth hanging on, for United became Champions of the Southern League in 1926/27. The league had by then been whittled down to fourteen teams and United beat off the other thirteen by virtue of their remarkable home record. They won twelve of their thirteen matches at Plainmoor, and it was that form which sent them to the top of the table. They finished on thirty eight points from twenty six matches — exactly the same as Bristol City Reserves. But United's goal average was marginally better, having scored sixty three and conceded thirty. Bristol City Reserves had scored more – seventy seven – but had let in thirty seven, so United just sneaked in ahead of them.

If the present system of goal difference had been in force, Bristol City would have won the league above United. On the basis of their surprise title, Torquay applied to join the Football League, and their application duly went to the vote of the league clubs.

The ballot proved as nail-biting as United's neck and neck title race; for the first time in the league's history the vote ended in a tie, with both United and Aberdare, who had finished bottom of the football league, polling twenty seven. So a re-run was held and United this time ousted Aberdare by a majority of seven, after extensive lobbying of the clubs by United Chairman, Charles Hore.

Torquay had the South Wales coal-mining depression to thank for their entry into the Football League. It was the decline of the mining industry following the 1926 General Strike that persuaded the league clubs that United were financially better suited to league football than the Welsh club, whose hard hit supporters could no longer afford to attend matches.

So it was that United found themselves in Football League Division Three (South) for the start of the 1927/28 season. Their decision the previous year to decline entry into the FA Cup competition to concentrate all their efforts on winning league status had more than paid off.

The step up proved too great for them at first — they finished bottom of the twenty two-club league which, interestingly, included Queens Park Rangers and Norwich as well as Plymouth Argyle and Exeter City. United's inaugural game in the league was, in fact, at home to neighbours Exeter on

Torquay United 1927/8 — their first year in the Football League. The picture was probably taken before their first game, a 1-1 draw with Exeter City at Plainmoor.

7

27 August 1927, when 11,625 people turned up to watch a 1-1 draw. United's first, historic goal in the league came from the penalty spot, with Herbert Turner doing the honours. The attendance that day was the biggest until after the war.

. After the honourable draw against Exeter, United got a taste of what they were in for in the very next game when they were trounced 9-1 at Millwall. The Magpies, as United were then known, went on to concede five goals on five other occasions later in the year. Their 'goals against' tally come the end of the season had reached a mind-boggling 103!

But there was no automatic relegation in those days and United lived to fight another season after successfully applying for re-election. It was another fifty seven years before Torquay faced the ignominy of seeking re-election again.

Full-back Percy Mackrill was player-manager in that first season — and he certainly had his hands full. But United plugged away despite their obvious difficulties in adapting to the higher league. United finished fourth from bottom in the 1929/30 season, when neighbours Plymouth won the league. The fixture between the two teams at Plainmoor on 4 September was a real thriller with Argyle sneaking a 4-3 win courtesy of a penalty-with-a-difference.

With the score at 3-3 and with 10,000 Devonians watching with baited breath, Argyle's goalkeeper walked the length of the pitch to take the penalty, which he duly converted.

It could never be claimed that United set the world alight in the years leading up to the war — their highest end of season position was tenth, where they finished two years running in 1935 and 1936. The man at the helm during the thirties was Frank Brown, who had the unusual title of trainer-manager.

Despite their early struggles, the club threw up several players who went on to bigger and better things. The big local discovery before the war was Ralph Birkett, an outside-right from Dartmouth. He made his debut for United at the age of seventeen, when he created all the seven goals they put past Bournemouth at Plainmoor on 8 May 1930. Twelve months later he scored his debut goal for Torquay — against Bournemouth.

Arsenal then paid the not insubstantial sum of £2,000 for Birkett, although he later moved on to Middlesbrough. While at Arsenal he linked up to form an all-Devon front line with Ray Bowden of Plymouth and Cliff Bastin of Exeter. He became the first Torquay-produced player to play for England, making his international debut in England's 3-1 win over Ireland in Belfast in October 1935.

Another United old-boy to win England honours was Don Welsh, who played centre-half at Plainmoor in the mid-thirties. Welsh was one of

United's all time greatest players before he moved on to Charlton Athletic. Yet he entered the football arena via an unusual route. A regular in the Royal Navy, he played soccer for the services at Devonport until Frank Brown spotted him and immediately offered to buy him out of the Navy. But complications arose when he was due to sail to China on a three-year commission on HMS Eagle.

The Navy then threw him a life-line and said that if he could find a replacement they would agree to release him. He had long since given up hope when he started up a conversation with a young man in a pub, who told him: "It's always been my ambition to visit China. I wish I was in your shoes." Hardly believing his good fortune, Welsh told the man he could have his shoes if he swapped places with him — which he did.

Such was the bizarre story behind United signing up the player who would have played many times for England had the war not intervened. As it was, Welsh represented his country three times after leaving Torquay for Charlton, who were then managed by Jimmy Seed. Welsh went on to lift the FA Cup for the London club just after the war.

It was not the only connection United had with FA Cup finalists in the ten years leading up to the out-break of World War II. Their goalkeeper between 1928 and 1930 was Harold Gough, who had kept goal for Sheffield United

Torquay United's 1928/9 line up, probably taken before the first game of the season — United's second in the League — a game United lost 4-3 at home to QPR.

9

in the last FA Cup final to be played before the First World War. He was reaching the end of his career and was a grey, middle-aged man by the time he called it a day at Torquay.

Meanwhile Babbacombe-born Sid Cann, who started his playing days at United, went on to play for Manchester City in the 1933 Cup Final against Everton. Cann, who played centre-half, represented England at schoolboy level during his career, which later took him to Southampton.

Another outstanding discovery during those pre-war years was Bert Head, who arrived at Plainmoor a complete unknown. An out-and-out stopper in the heart of defence, he was one of many players whose career was wrecked by the war. After his playing days he turned to management and masterminded Crystal Palace's climb from the Third Division to the First.

Plainmoor was not short of characters during the thirties and another on the list was Les Lievesley, a free transfer signing from Manchester United. He moved to Turin where he became team coach after the war, but was killed in a plane crash which was responsible for wiping out the entire Turin side.

United's defensive back-bone in the years after the war — (L to R): Bert Head, Phil Joslin, Bob Keeton.

Off the pitch, United's home crowds hovered around the 4,000 mark. Some would-be fans were put off by United's erratic form during the decade, which saw them avoid bottom position, only narrowly, on no fewer than five occasions. But, if nothing else, being a United follower was always fun. The 1931/32 season witnessed such bizarre defeats as 10-2 at Fulham, 7-0 at Crystal Palace, 6-3 at Watford, and 6-1 at Luton. Yet it also saw United thrash Bristol Rovers 8-1 at Plainmoor! And, as if to prove the earlier 10-2 defeat was no fluke, United emulated the feat in September 1933, this time at Luton.

The war interrupted proceedings and United reconvened at the start of the 1945/46 war-time League season, when Billy Butler was manager. In United's first game of that war-time season, England's centre-half at the time, Neil Franklin, guested for them against Bristol Rovers at Plainmoor. Franklin's presence did not prevent United losing 3-0 however. The Football League proper did not re-assemble until the following (1946/47) season, when Butler was replaced as manager by his namesake, former United player Jack Butler.

The Torquay side after the war boasted Ireland's international goalkeeper, Jerry Matier. Also appearing for United in the following years was Cornishman Mike Tiddy, who went on to play outside-right for Arsenal and England Under-23's.

The latter years of the 1940s decade in fact brought with them the arrival of some of the best players ever to play for United. Dennis Lewis made his debut in 1947 and he still holds the record for most appearances in a Torquay shirt to this day. He played 433 times on the right wing and then at right-half for the club before finally calling it a day in 1959. And to think United snapped him up on a free transfer from Swansea City!

In 1948, United signed inside forward Don Mills on loan from Queens Park Rangers. He departed at the end of the season, only to return to Plainmoor again two years later. Mills was the greatest player ever to play

Some of United's all-time greats at a benefit match against Southampton in April 1950. (L to R): Jack Conley, Sid Cann, Ralph Calland, Don Mills, Phil Joslin, Bob John (Manager).

11

The team which faced First Division Huddersfield in the fourth round of the FA Cup in 1955 in front of 21,908 fans at Plainmoor: (L to R) Back row: Bill Towers, Dennis Lewis, Eric Webber, Alf Jeffries, Geoff Norman, Harry Smith, Dave Pryde (trainer). Front row: Ron Shaw, Sammy Collins, Harold Dobbie, Don Mills, Jack Smith.

for United and was probably the most talented footballer in the lower divisions at the time.

In the same year Sammy Collins made his debut for United, although it was not until a few years later that he established himself as a prolific goal-scorer.

Meanwhile South Devon was still carrying on its tradition of producing its own crop of talented young players and one of them, goalkeeper Peter Wakeham, was sold to north-east giants Sunderland.

United's already impressive forward line was further supplemented by the so-called 'Wizard on the Wing' Ronnie Shaw. He, along with Mills, Collins and Lewis, made an immediate impact at the turnstiles and the visit of Plymouth Argyle on 7 October 1950, brought the biggest crowd ever to watch a league match at Plainmoor — 16,388. They witnessed United win the Devon derby 3-2.

The record crowd ever to attend a Plainmoor fixture however was in 1955, when a staggering 21,908 turned out to see Huddersfield win an FA Cup fourth round tie 1-0. The manager behind what some feel was United's best ever side was Eric Webber, who started off as player-manager in 1951 before

Harold Dobbie lies beaten and Jack Smith moves in to rob a Huddersfield Town player in front of Plainmoor's record crowd.

concentrating solely on the managerial side of things. Little did anyone suspect that he would remain at the helm for another fourteen years — a minor miracle in football management terms.

One of Torquay United's most endearing, not to mention infuriating, characteristics is their unpredictability. Just a quick glance at their performances during the 1940s and 1950s shows they finished as high as fifth on two occasions and as low as twenty first.

Unfortunately for United, they finished twenty first in the year the present league system was introduced, so they found themselves kicking off the 1958/59 season in the newly created Football League Division Four.

Yet it could have been so much different just twelve months earlier, when United reached their highest ever league position and missed out on promotion to Division Two by the narrowest of margins — a decimal point. The team which beat them on goal average was Alf Ramsey's Ipswich Town, who had just started their charge to the First Division. United had actually thrashed Ipswich 4-1 at Plainmoor on the opening day of the 1956/57 season, with two goals from Mills and one a-piece from Shaw and John Anderton. Ipswich gained their revenge and a bit more in the return game at Portman Road on 15 December however, beating United 6-0.

The promotion race all boiled down to the very last day of the season, when

Torquay United FC — 1956/7. (L to R) Back row: D. Pryde (trainer), G. Norman, G. Northcott, P. Wakeman, J. James, J. Smith, H. Dobbie. Front row: R. Shaw, D. Lewis, S. Collins, E. Calland, D. Mills, A. Collins.

Torquay found themselves needing to win at struggling Crystal Palace to be sure of going up. United had won their penultimate game 3-0 at home to Queens Park Rangers, while Ipswich could only manage a 3-3 draw with Southend United. Those two results meant United jumped one point above the Suffolk club with both teams going into their final game of the season on Monday, 1 May.

United's hopes of a win were dashed when Palace took an early lead, but they were raised again shortly afterwards when Jimmy James equalised. It set up a tense finish, with United camped in the Palace half. But the goal which would have put them into the Second Division for the first time in their history just would not come. Eric Webber had recalled Don Mills for the game after he had missed the encounter with QPR a few days earlier through injury. Mills came in for Ted Calland, who had scored fifteen goals in twenty nine games that season. Some feel Mills was not fully fit and that United might have won had Calland played.

The draw meant United's fate was all down to how Ipswich had fared at Southampton with United and Webber hoping his former club had done them a favour by at least taking a point off Ramsey's side. But the bad news filtered through that Ipswich had not slipped up like Torquay had done, winning 2-0. That left the top of the table looking like this:

	Pl	For	Ag	Pts
Ipswich Town	46	101	54	59
Torquay Utd	46	89	64	59

It meant that, after the goal average had been worked out, United had failed to win promotion by a decimal point.

On a lighter note, one of the quirkiest statistics of the season involved United's league clashes with Millwall. Astonishingly, both fixtures ended up 7-2! United won at Plainmoor and Millwall exacted their revenge by exactly the same scoreline at The Den.

Torquay United pictured in 1957. (L to R) Back row: Horace Langstreth, John Smith, Peter Wakeham, Mervyn Gill, Harry Smith, John Anderton. Middle Row: Harold Kellow (physio), Jimmy James, Ron Newman, Dennis Lewis, Alan Smith, George Northcott, Nobby Clarke, Jack Smith, Dave Pryde (trainer). Front row: Eric Johnson, Sammy Collins, Colin Bettany, Eric Webber (Manager), Don Mills, Ron Shaw, Graham Bond.

Meanwhile, the post war years marked the start of a long line of prolific goalscorers at Torquay — a line which continued right up until the 1970s, when the dearth eventually set in.

2. GOALSCORERS

It was not until after the war that Torquay became blessed with a series of truly prolific goal-scorers. Even so, United possessed several forwards and midfielders during the 1930s who could all be relied upon to hit the back of the net at regular intervals.

One who certainly fell into that category was Jimmy Trotter, who joined United from Sheffield Wednesday towards the end of his career. Trotter had an astonishing strike-rate in his first season at Plainmoor, netting twenty five goals in just thirty eight games in 1930/31. He went on to add a further ten goals the following season.

His departure coincided with the advent at Plainmoor of Paignton's George Stabb, who was United's leading scorer for the next two years. He hit twenty four in forty appearances in 1932/33 and added another thirteen the following year. Then, after scoring four in five games in the autumn of 1934, Stabb, along with United's outside-right Ernie Steele, was sold to Notts County.

Torquay United's top goalscorer in the 1949/50 season, Jack Conley, puts pressure on the Millwall goalkeeper in United's 1-0 victory on 17 December 1949.

The goal-scoring task was then handed to Ben Morton, who was signed from Manchester United. He made an immediate impact at Plainmoor, netting twenty three goals in his first season in 1936/37. He was also United's leading scorer the next year, this time with ten goals in only twelve appearances. Then, to the immense disappointment of club and fans alike, United, dogged by financial problems, had to sell Morton to Swindon Town to raise some much-needed cash.

The man responsible for scoring more goals than anyone else during the pre-war decade, however, was Albert Hutchinson. Sheffield-born Hutchinson was a free-scoring inside-left who later moved to left-half and finally ended his career at left-back.

He proved to be one of United's greatest ever servants and played in all nine seasons in the 1930s, scoring eighty one goals in the process. He was ever-present in both the 1930/31 and 1931/32 seasons. He made many goals from his inside-left position, but he was also the club's top marksman for two years running in the mid-thirties. He netted nineteen goals in 1934/35 and another ten the following season.

And then there was the incomparable Sammy Collins who joined United in 1948 and for three seasons partnered another of Plainmoor's great strikers, Jack Conley, to form the most lethal partnership the club has ever had.

Sammy Collins doing what he did best — aiming for goal — in United's 1-1 draw at home to Crystal Palace in August 1955, their first home game of the season. Watching is Harold Dobbie, who scored United's goal that day.

Those post-war years heralded the arrival of a string of top-class forwards — and it was Collins and Conley who started off a wonderful era for United in front of goal. Conley was the club's leading scorer in the 1946/47 season with twenty three goals and he held the same title two years later, this time scoring nineteen goals. He was one of the best headers of the ball ever to play for the club and in his five years at Plainmoor scored a total of sixty seven league goals.

United's 'Wing Wizard', Ronnie Shaw, lets fly during their 2-0 home win against Walsall in September 1954, watched by Harold Dobbie. This was in the days before goalkeepers wore gloves!

Collins and Conley were joined by United's best winger of all time, Ron Shaw, and the trio linked up to form an awesome front-line. Although Shaw created many of Torquay's goals between 1946 and 1958, he could also be relied upon to add a fair few himself. In fact, he came tantalisingly close to a goalscoring century during his twelve years with United, hitting the target ninety nine times.

United seemed to have an endless stream of reliable strikers during the immediate post-war era. Their most accomplished player at the time, and probably of all time, Don Mills, netted eighty one goals in 342 appearances for Torquay from his inside-left position. But it was Collins who made most

Opposite Page: The legendary Stanley Matthews (third right) guested for Torquay United in a floodlit friendly against Blackburn Rovers in 1955. (L to R) Back row: Dennis Lewis, Jack Smith, Norman Lloyd, Don Mills. Front row: John Smith, Dave Pryde (trainer), Eric Webber, Harold Dobbie, Sammy Collins, Stanley Matthews, Bill Hayes, Harry Smith.

of the headlines during the fifties, and he still holds the Torquay United goal-scoring record with 204 goals in the ten years between 1948 and 1958. It is hard to imagine that total ever being bettered.

Collins' year by year record:
1948/49: 13 goals in 22 league games
1949/50: 12 goals in 23 league games
1950/51: 11 goals in 26 league games
1951/52: 22 goals in 42 league games
1952/53: 27 goals in 44 league games
1953/54: 17 goals in 40 league games
1954/55: 26 goals in 45 league games
1955/56: 40 goals in 45 league games
1956/57: 30 goals in 46 league games
1957/58: 6 goals in 24 league games

Collins' forty-goal tally in 1955 is still a club record and represents almost a goal a game. He hit no fewer than *five* hat-tricks and hit a double on four other occasions during that goals-all-the-way season. In fact, he scored more goals single-handedly that year than the entire team put together could manage in the 1984/85 season. Collins was United's top scorer for seven consecutive seasons between 1950/51 and 1956/57.

Collins, who now lives in Bristol, was an old-fashioned inside-forward, lightning quick in and around the penalty area. United's goal tally during the 1950s was remarkable, particularly when compared to today's standards — they totalled eighty six goals in 1951/52; eighty seven in 1952/53; eighty one the following season; eighty two during 1954/55; eighty six in 1955/56; and eighty nine in 1956/57. If United's defence hadn't done such a good impression of a sieve during those years, they would surely have won promotion to Division Two. A prime example of such leaky tendencies came in the 1951/52 season, when they conceded ninety eight goals!

United fans had not mourned the loss of Sammy Collins long before they had a new hero. And what's more the prolific young Tommy Northcott was a local hero, hailing from Hele Village. He played for Hele Rovers before turning professional at the age of seventeen in 1950. He scored ten goals for United before being transferred to Cardiff City in 1952, only to return to Plainmoor five years later after a spell with Lincoln City.

Northcott, who played alongside his elder brother George at Plainmoor, is widely thought to be one of the best players to have come out of Torquay — and his goals played a big part in United's promotion year in 1959/60. They were also instrumental in keeping United in the Third Division until 1963. Northcott netted 125 goals between 1957 and 1966, when he was released by manager Frank O'Farrell at the end of United's promotion season.

Northcott was an intelligent, quick thinking centre-forward, quite often one thought and one step ahead of his opposing defenders. His talent was recognised early on in his career, when he was selected to represent England's youth team.

United players training during the 1957/8 season — the year they finished 21st in Division 3 (South). (L to R) Harry Smith, Eric Johnson, Griff Norman, Dennis Lewis, Jimmy James, Don Mills, Larry Baxter, Colin Bettany, Tommy Northcott, Mervyn Gill.

Despite Sammy Collins' invincible record, it is probably Robin Stubbs that most supporters remember best. When he was brought to Plainmoor from Birmingham City for £6,000 in 1963, United were again languishing in Division Four after a brief interlude in the Third Division. It was his goals which were largely responsible for revitalising the club's fortunes and put United on the verge of promotion in 1964 — and then helped them to win promotion two years later.

Robin, who is now a salesman in Torquay, was an English striker in the traditional mould. He was a great believer in the adage that it is better to stick to what you do best. On that basis, he did nothing else but score goals. He all-but ignored the rest of the pitch and concentrated all his efforts on what went on in the opposition's penalty area.

Those deadly goal-scoring instincts helped him to net 120 league goals between 1963 and 1969. He was the club's leading scorer for five of those seasons and in his two most prolific years between 1963 and 1965, he scored twenty four and thirty one goals respectively. And his three year partnership up front with Tommy Northcott yielded 100 goals exactly, making them one of the most feared duos in the lower divisions.

Stubbs' five goals in United's 8-3 trouncing of Newport County in October 1963 is still a club record for goals scored in one match. Astonishingly, six of those Torquay goals came in the last nineteen minutes!

United's 'Golden Boy' of the 1960s, Robin Stubbs, playing in the celebrity game before the Sherpa Van Final at Wembley

Stubbs will always be remembered for his two late goals in United's FA Cup third round tie against First Division giants Tottenham Hotspur in January 1965. United, 1-3 down at Plainmoor and with just five minutes left to play, looked down and out against the club which had achieved the League and Cup double just four years earlier. But Robin's two last-gasp goals earned United a replay at White Hart Lane, which Spurs duly won 5-1.

Somewhat surprisingly, the year Torquay finished fourth in Division Three in 1968, Stubbs only scored nine goals in thirty starts. Yet he was still the highest scorer as thirteen others contributed to United's goal tally of sixty.

He left Plainmoor at the end of the 1968/69 season to join Bristol Rovers — only to return to Torquay three years later. He started nine matches in the 1972/73 season, but scored only once and was forced to retire from the game shortly afterwards, the victim of a severe knee injury — ten years after he had first arrived at Plainmoor.

"My second spell with Torquay was a waste of time for both myself and the club," recalls Robin now. "I had a bad knee and I never really recovered from it — I wasn't fit during my second spell."

But he remembers the sixties as a much happier time: "Playing for Torquay with the side we had during the sixties was wonderful. We had some great players — especially the West Ham lads Frank O'Farrell brought down to Plainmoor like Ken Brown and John Bond. And it was always a great feeling to run out onto the pitch knowing there would be 9,000 or more people in the ground."

He is also quick to pay tribute to his striking partner in the early and mid-sixties, Tommy Northcott: "He was an excellent player to play alongside — and he certainly took a lot of kicks laying the ball on to me! We only played together for three years, but it was a very profitable era in front of goal and we complimented each other very well. Unfortunately our partnership didn't last that long because Tommy was coming towards the end of his career at Torquay."

Robin hints that he would have liked to have had the opportunity to display his obvious goal-scoring talents at a higher level when he says: "I nearly left Torquay on a number of occasions for various reasons during the sixties but didn't — again, for various reasons."

He still watches United when his job permits, and he found himself playing in a Torquay United shirt again in May 1989, this time in a team of 'Golden Oldies' before the Sherpa Van Trophy final at Wembley. "It was the best day out I've had for a long time — a real experience and I was delighted to be asked."

Stubbs was United's last truly prolific striker. A downturn in the club's fortunes naturally coincided with a similar downturn in their goal-scoring record.

Even so, the last twenty years has thrown up several strikers who, if not in the same league as Collins or Stubbs, did none the less leave their mark.

In the two seasons between 1969 and 1971 the front partnership of Alan Welsh and John Rudge notched fifty five goals between them. The following year, 1972, United were relegated to the Fourth Division and, during the years which followed, goals were relatively few and far between.

The mid-seventies saw the arrival of diminutive Scotsman Willie Brown, who became United's top goal-getter in the three seasons between 1975 and 1978, netting fourteen, eighteen, and twelve goals respectively. Short and stocky, Brown was as untypical a striker as Stubbs was typical.

He was followed by United's best striker since Robin Stubbs ten years earlier — Steve Cooper. He totalled seventy five league goals for the club between 1977 and 1984. A rare Fourth Division number nine, he was both good in the air and on the ground. The latter part of his career was dogged by injury, which eventually forced him out of league football. The year after his departure, United's goal tally was the worst in their history — just thirty eight in the 1984/85 season when they finished bottom of the league. In fact, the highest scorer that year was teenager Mario Walsh with a paltry five.

Although he was only at Plainmoor for two years, Paul Dobson left his indelible mark at the club. He will, of course, be forever remembered as the man who saved the club from non-league oblivion.

Up until 4.46 pm on Saturday, 9 May 1987, Dobbo had scored fifteen goals in thirty league starts during the season. Yet those goals still did not seem enough to save an apparently doomed United who, trailing 1-2 at home to Crewe on the last day of the season, were on their way out of the Football League.

But in the fourth minute of injury time Dobson, ever the opportunist, capitalised on a mix-up in the Crewe Alexandra defence and, with his back to goal, turned and hit a low shot into the far corner of the net. He was not to know it at the time, but that goal was enough to keep United in the league on goal difference and condemn Lincoln to the Vauxhall Conference League — they were simultaneously losing at Swansea City.

Of all the 1,749 goals United had scored since the inception of the Fourth Division, none had been more important — and it was enough to make Dobbo a Plainmoor legend.

He added a further twenty two league goals the following season, when United narrowly missed out on promotion. Sadly for United, home-sick Dobbo left the club at the end of that 1987/88 season to return to his native north.

In May 1989, Dean Edwards made history by becoming the first United player ever to score at Wembley. His 23rd-minute header, which gave Torquay a brief lead against Bolton Wanderers in the Sherpa Van Trophy Final, may not have been enough to win the game but, just like Dobson's two years earlier, will always be etched in the memories of all Gulls' followers.

In the 1989/90 season, striker Carl Airey equalled Sammy Collins' record set during the 1954/55 season of scoring in seven successive league matches, before his season was brought to a premature end by a knee injury.

Meanwhile, local lad Mark Loram could go on to become one of the club's top scorers — if he remains at Plainmoor. Having made his debut as a seventeen year old in the 1984/85 season, he has since scored nearly fifty goals for the club. That total would have been higher had his United days not been interrupted by a spell with First Division Queens Park Rangers before he returned to live in his home town of Brixham.

3. THE GLORY YEARS 1959-1971

Torquay United did not take long to get out of the newly created Football League Division Four, although the omens from the first year were not too promising. After winning their inaugural game 2-0 at Chester thanks to two goals from Geoff Cox, United had one of their frustratingly up and down years. They had good wins over Barrow, Workington and Southport that year — all of whom have since gone out of the league. United finished the season in mid-table and were put in the shade somewhat by local rivals Exeter City who, after finishing bottom of Division Three (South) the previous year, only just missed out on promotion. The two Devon clubs fought out two exciting battles that season, drawing 2-2 at St James' Park, while City won a 4-3 thriller at Plainmoor. Local boy Tommy Northcott was ever-present in United's forty six league fixtures and accounted for twenty of their seventy eight goals.

After finishing a respectable, if not earth-shattering twelfth in the first year, United, managed by Eric Webber, sneaked promotion the next, finishing third behind Walsall and Notts County in May 1960. Their run-in was not as nerve-wracking as it might have been because of their virtual infallibility at home — and because of their consistency during the second half of the season. In twenty one games after the turn of the year, United won eleven, drew six and lost just four.

Their twenty six league wins that season is still a club record, while their goal-tally in the forty six matches was an impressive eighty four.

United had all but sewn up promotion well before the last game of the season. The penultimate weekend saw them take a giant step towards the Third Division when they came from behind to beat Crystal Palace 2-1 at Plainmoor. The 7,217 crowd were stunned into silence in the fifteenth minute when John Gavin gave the London club a surprise lead. Fears that United were about to throw away their golden opportunity to get out of the basement league were dispelled when Graham Bond and Tommy Northcott grabbed the two second half goals which kept them on course for promotion.

It left United needing just one point from their last three matches and it set them up nicely for the midweek game at home to Gillingham. Needing only a point, United went one better, winning 2-0 on 27 April 1960, to make Third Division football a certainty — just three years after the heart-ache of missing out on promotion to Division Two by a decimal point. The win was secured by goals from Graham Bond and Colin Court.

With all the nerves gone, United went on to draw their last two games — 2-2 at Bradford and 1-1 at Barrow. They had clinched third spot, three points clear of nearest rivals Watford!

That year saw two local brothers playing alongside each other. Striker Tommy Northcott, who scored fifteen goals, joined his elder brother George, who played at centre-half. The pair went on to play in the same side for the next two seasons as well.

United defending during their 3-1 away win at Bournemouth in October 1960 — their first year back in Division Three. (L to R) Don Mills, Colin Rawson, Mervyn Gill (goalkeeper), Colin Bettany, George Northcott, Dennis Penford.

United's success that season had much to do with the performances in defence by Colin Bettany, a right-back, who also played at centre-half. He was ever present, playing in all forty six league games. Remarkably, he was also an ever-present fixture in the side for the following three seasons as well.

Any dreams United may have had of achieving Second Division football were dashed the next year when, in a dreadful run-in, Torquay could manage just two wins in their last nineteen fixtures. The defence was positively leaking goals — letting in six at Bury and five at Coventry City in consecutive matches. United's last four games were no better either, losing 4-2 at Grimsby, 6-1 at home to Queens Park Rangers, 3-1 at Swindon Town and 5-1 at Reading — quite a sequence! It was possibly just as well United were safe enough half-way up the league for the dreadful finale not to matter. Yet it was a sign of what was to follow.

Off the pitch, 1960 saw the arrival on the Board of Directors of local solicitor Mr Tony Boyce, who was later to become the Chairman and who is now President of the club.

The 1961/62 season was a real nail-biter and ended with United reacquainting themselves with the Fourth Division by going down on the very last day of the season.

United only needed a draw at Barnsley to stay up and send the Yorkshire club down. And they looked well on the way to safety when they took a 2-1 lead through goals by Gordon Astall and Brian Handley. But disaster struck as Barnsley, obviously awoken from their stupor, went on to score three more goals to condemn Torquay to the lower division for the start of the 1962/63 season.

What made the defeat even more galling was that United had thrashed Barnsley 6-2 when the two sides had met at Plainmoor in September that season.

That result apart, it was another season of horrific results, notably the 6-0 defeat at Queens Park Rangers, obviously carrying on from where they had left off the previous year, and the 7-2 thrashing at Crystal Palace. United conceded 106 goals in their forty six league fixtures in the 1961/62 relegation season.

They finished fourth from bottom on thirty six points — two less than both Barnsley and Shrewsbury Town.

United's greatest all-time player, Don Mills, used the occasion to hang up his boots to become the club's assistant trainer — fourteen years after he first arrived at Plainmoor.

The next two years proved to be frustrating ones for United, finishing sixth and just missing out on a return to Division Three in both the 1962/63 and 1963/64 seasons. They had a dream start to their first year back in the Fourth Division, beating local rivals Exeter City 3-0 at St James' Park, thanks to an Ernie Pym hat-trick. It seemed for a while that United were on their way back to the Third Division at the first attempt. But despite winning four of their last five games, they were just pipped for a promotion spot, finishing a tantalising three points behind Oldham Athletic in second and Crewe Alexandra in third position. United in fact lost fewer games than any other team in the division that season — ten.

Manager Webber, under increasing pressure to lift United out of the Fourth Division, invested a club record fee of £6,000 for Birmingham City striker Robin Stubbs for the 1963/64 season, desperately hoping he would fill the elusive missing part of the jig-saw. And what an inspired signing it proved to be!

Stubbs repaid that fee with interest. Playing only thirty four games that season, he hit twenty four of United's league goals. His partnership with Northcott in the early sixties was one of the most feared in the division. Yet United still missed out on promotion, largely because of their dreadful end to the season.

United were left to rue their Jekyll and Hyde nature — they were in sparkling form at home, but unpredictable to say the least away from Plainmoor. United looked to have the Third Division in their sights before Christmas when, in an eleven match winning streak at Plainmoor, they thrashed everyone in sight. That run saw them win some thrillers, the highlights of which were the 8-3 win over Newport, the 6-2 win against Bradford, and the 5-0 drubbing of Chester.

Robin Stubbs was sent off along with the then Oxford player Ron Atkinson — for fighting during their match at The Manor Ground on Boxing Day, a game Oxford won 1-0.

If United's away form had been anything like it was at Plainmoor, they would have run away with the league, but they just could not reproduce their goal-happy performances while on their travels. The final nail in the promotion coffin came during the last eleven matches, when United could only scramble one, solitary victory. It again meant United had just missed out, when at one point, they had looked almost certain to go up.

The following year, 1964/65, was the last season in charge for manager Eric Webber, who was sacked, somewhat harshly, after fourteen years at Plainmoor on 3 May 1965 — just five days after United's last game of the season. Torquay had a poor season in the league compared to their previous two years and ended in mid-table, despite another thirty one goals from Stubbs and eleven from Northcott.

The year was brightened up by United's FA Cup exploits, when they so nearly upset mighty Spurs, who then had Alan Mullery, Alan Gilzean, the incomparable Jimmy Greaves and a certain Cyril Knowles in their side. The crowd of more than 20,000 which packed the tiny Plainmoor ground on 9 January 1965, witnessed a shock in the making when Bill Atkinson gave United the lead from the penalty spot after Stubbs had been brought down by Knowles.

Tommy Northcott climbs above Alan Mullery during the 3-3 draw in the FA Cup tie against mighty Spurs in January 1965. Watching, in the background, for United is Geoff Cox.

Yet they could not have been all that surprised when Tottenham recovered to take a 3-1 lead with two goals from Gilzean and another from Maurice Norman. The game seemed dead and buried with only five minutes to go, but Spurs were in for the shock of their lives.

Stubbs set up a tremendous finale when he hit a deflected shot into the Spurs net to make it 3-2. Then, two minutes later, it was a case of *déja-vu* as Stubbs hit another fluke into the net, the ball coming off his leg as he stuck out a boot to block a clearance. That was the cue for hundreds of disbelieving fans to mount a spontaneous pitch invasion and the game was held up while the playing area was cleared.

When the game eventually resumed, United pounded the Spurs goal and only desperate defending kept United's by-now rampaging forwards at bay. So a relieved Spurs lived to fight another day, but Robin Stubbs doubts they would have survived another five minutes of such relentless pressure: "We weren't in it for most of the match, but we were all over them come the end. Another five minutes and I think we would have got the winner."

And he admitted he had Lady Luck to thank for both of his goals: "The first one was deflected and the second one was a blocked tackle. I stuck my foot out and the ball rebounded and went off in a banana shape into the corner of the net — beautifully placed! My aim on both occasions was to find the back of the net, and in that sense I succeeded. In fact, I could have had a hat-trick that day had it not been for a late change of mind. I was down to take the penalties, but I'd missed a couple recently and I was fed up with getting the blame — so I handed the job over to Bill Atkinson and he took the penalties after that."

Thousands of hopeful Torquay supporters headed up to London for the replay, only to find that the game had been postponed due to a waterlogged pitch. The 4,000 fans repeated their trek a week later and watched Spurs turn on the style to win 5-1. Greaves gave them the lead, only for Stubbs to shock them again by hitting an equaliser. Two more goals from Greaves and one each from Gilzean and Jimmy Robertson ended United's cup hopes for that year. The 55,081 spectators who attended the replay at White Hart Lane is the largest crowd ever to watch a match involving Torquay.

The Spurs games, along with Stubbs' thirty one league goals were the only things to lighten up United's year. Their 2-1 win at Wrexham on the last day of the season on 28 April 1965, marked the end of an era as it was Webber's last game in charge of the club. The board felt that, having finished in mid-table, the time was right for a new face to take over.

Webber had been a loyal servant of Torquay, joining them in 1951 as player-manager before becoming manager in 1955. He had been in charge of United's great side of the fifties, which boasted the best players ever to play at Plainmoor. And the sacking came as a great shock to Webber himself:

"I couldn't believe it when I was dismissed," recalls Eric, who now lives in Southampton. "I expected to be kept on and I certainly wasn't surprised that I had stayed at Plainmoor for as long as fourteen years. I loved the club and the area and was very unhappy at having to leave. They were very happy days. We had outstanding players like Sammy Collins, Ronnie Shaw, John Benson—and the greatest of them all, Don Mills. I used to shout at the other players just to get the ball on to Don's left foot and he used to shout back 'I can use the other bugger as well'. Then, in the sixties we had everyone's favourite, Robin Stubbs and Tommy Northcott, who was also a great player, but not as popular as he should have been."

Eric Webber gives a tactical team talk in November 1951. (L to R) Eric Webber, Sammy Collins, George Webber, Dave Topping, Marwood Marchant, Ellis Stuttard, John Reid, Ron Shaw, Bill Thomas, Henry McGuinness, Ralph Calland.

Not surprisingly, apart from being sacked, Eric's biggest disappointment was missing out on promotion in the 1956/57 season by a decimal point. "I couldn't believe how well Crystal Palace played in the last game of the season. I was hoping my old club Southampton, where I'd left to join Torquay, had done us a favour—but they hadn't. That year was the biggest disappointment in my footballing career. Not getting back into the Third Division in the two or three years before I left was also sad because we so

United line-up in 1953/4. (L to R) Back row: Dennis Lewis, Harry Parfitt, George Webber, Bill Hayes, Jimmy Drinkwater, George Northcott. Middle row: Harold Kellow (physio), a reserve team player, Bill Towers, Henry McGuinness, Griff Norman, Albert Calland, another reserve team player, Dave Pryde (trainer). Front row: Norman Lloyd, Ron Shaw, Sammy Collins, Eric Webber (Manager), Don Mills, Bill Thomas, Ernie Edds.

nearly did it on a couple of occasions. Then getting the sack was, in my opinion, the wrong decision."

Eric had open-heart surgery in 1979, but has now recovered well and is enjoying life at the age of seventy — even if he doesn't always understand modern football: "I used to tell my players to get the ball, and once they had the ball, I would tell them to aim for the opposition's goal. I'm not sure whether that is always the case now. And I have trouble following the game these days because I can never work out who is playing where."

Having outlined his biggest disappointments, Eric recalls the cup-run in 1954/55 as his favourite memory: "Drawing at Leeds and then beating them 4-0 in the third round replay was wonderful — as was getting over 21,000 fans in to watch the next round against Huddersfield." And he added: "Thinking back, I gave my life to Torquay United, football-wise." Yet he was not given an invitation to join other United 'old boys' at the Wembley final in 1989.

If his departure marked the end of an era, it also signalled the start of a new

31

one, when Weymouth manager Frank O'Farrell was appointed new manager by Tony Boyce for the start of the 1965/66 season. The appointment was somewhat controversial, with many believing United should have chosen a more experienced manager.

While the nation's eyes were focused on England's glorious World Cup campaign, it went virtually unnoticed, except to United followers, that Torquay won promotion to the Third Division in the summer of '66. United's first game of the season, when they lost 4-1 at Bradford, proved merely to be a temporary aberration — certainly no signs there of what was to come.

Torquay won the next four games and went on to achieve twenty four victories that season. The vital last fifteen games of the season saw them win seven, draw four and lose four. It was enough to earn them third spot on fifty eight points, behind Doncaster and Darlington, who each had fifty nine. It was a tense run-in however, and Colchester, Tranmere and Luton finished just two points adrift of United. The 2-0 win at Colchester on 30 April not only avenged the 1-0 defeat they had suffered against them three weeks earlier, it ultimately provided United with their two-point advantage, over Colchester, Tranmere and Luton.

In fact United were only placed fifth as late as 23 April, four points behind Colchester.

Colchester	52 pts
Doncaster	51 pts
Darlington	51 pts
Chester	50 pts
Torquay	48 pts

United had to make a late push to get one of the top three spots — and that is precisely what they did. Their home game with Notts County on Monday, 9 May was the crunch game, one United simply had to win. And win they did, with goals from John Benson and Tommy Spratt giving them a vital 2-0 win. United then had a three week wait before their final game at Darlington on 21 May.

A thousand nervous United fans made the long trip to the North East for the game against the team lying in second position. United earned a 0-0 draw to secure promotion. As it happened, they would have been promoted even if they had lost because other results went in their favour, but they were not to know that, of course. Thousands of people lined the Newton Road the following day to cheer the team-coach home. After four seasons in the Fourth Division, United had made it back to the Third.

Doncaster	59 pts
Darlington	59 pts
Torquay	58 pts
Colchester	56 pts

United's success came despite losing goalkeeper Terry Adlington after only seventeen games of the season with a broken finger. O'Farrell was desperately searching for an adequate replacement when he received a letter from Gary McGuire, an amateur 'keeper offering his services. O'Farrell took up the offer and McGuire made sixteen appearances in the crucial last third of the season.

Up front, United had a lethal strike force with Spratt scoring eighteen and Stubbs adding another seventeen. In all, United found the back of the net seventy two times in that promotion season.

O'Farrell, a former West Ham player, used his contacts to bring down a whole series of Hammers' players. At one stage, there were seven of them at Plainmoor at the same time.

Somewhat controversially, O'Farrell introduced the sweeper system, employing the consistent John Benson for that role. It led to accusations from some quarters of defensive tactics, something which is refuted by Stubbs: "Frank was certainly a contrast to Eric Webber. You could not have had two more contrasting managers. Eric was, above all things a nice bloke.

"Frank came in and decided things had to be done. He was a disciplinarian, and in hindsight, he had a point. We needed that to achieve success. He also decided that we should play with a sweeper and it worked for us. He pulled a player out of attack and the system was effective in the lower divisions. Frank brought a lot of good players to Plainmoor especially the West Ham lads, and the spectators appreciated the way we played because there were always about 9,000 watching our home matches."

The introduction of substitutions during the promotion year enabled Geoff Cox to go down in history as the first United player to come on as sub during the 1-0 win at Doncaster on 2 October 1965.

United finished their first year back in Division Three in a creditable seventh place. It was a season punctuated by a series of bizarre results.

United started well enough, beating Reading 3-0 at Plainmoor. They also beat Walsall 5-2, Workington 5-1 and both Colchester and Brighton 5-0. But then again, they also lost 5-0 at Oldham, 4-0 at Middlesborough and 4-2 at home to Swansea City.

Unfortunately, those defeats at the hands of Middlesborough and Swansea came in the last two games of the season and were enough to thwart United's push for promotion. They ended up just three points behind third placed Watford — two wins in those last two disastrous games would have earned United promotion to the Second Division.

But what was to happen the following year was even more agonising with United finishing fourth in Division Three in May 1968 — yet it should have been even better.

United finished two points behind Shrewsbury Town in third place, after earlier being in the driving seat. United were featured on BBC TV's *Match of the Day* for the first time on 16 March when the nation watched them open up a five-point lead at the top of the table by beating Bury 3-0 at Plainmoor. It made United odds-on for promotion but, disastrously, they then lost three games in a row during April.

And, just like the previous year, they again lost the vital last two games of the season — 2-0 at Scunthorpe and 4-0 at Reading. From a seemingly unassailable position, United had thrown it all away right at the end. The top of the table at the end of the season looked like this:

Oxford	57 pts
Bury	56 pts
Shrewsbury	55 pts
Torquay	53 pts

It made agonising reading for United fans.

During the season, O'Farrell brought West Ham's centre-half Ken Brown to Plainmoor — two years after he had helped the Hammers win the European Cup Winners' Cup in 1965. He of course joined up with other West Ham old boys, including John Bond, and the two were to continue their association in a managerial capacity at Norwich City.

United went international just prior to the 1967/68 season when they embarked on their first ever Continental tour. They returned home unbeaten from the mini-tour of West Germany. They played four games, beating Dorsten 5-1 and Lippstadt 2-0, and drawing 1-1 with both Bayer Leverkusen and Bonner Sports Club.

The biggest story of the following (1968/69) season, came on Friday, December 13th. Then, it was announced that O'Farrell had been appointed new manager of First Division Leicester City, whom he led to the FA Cup Final just a few months later, when they lost 1-0 against Joe Mercer's Manchester City.

O'Farrell's league record in three and a half seasons at Plainmoor was: Played 160, won 76, drawn 34, lost 50. Goals for stood at 235, while goals against were 182. Of course, it was not the last we were to see of Frank, who was to return to Plainmoor for two further spells in the late 1970s and early 1980s.

Frank, who lives in Torquay, is still grateful to United for giving him his big break in league management: "I'd had four successful years at Weymouth. We won the Southern League and reached the fourth round of the FA Cup, so I was not unduly surprised when Tony Boyce approached me. I had recently applied for the manager's job at Watford and Colchester, and didn't get them, so I was delighted when United came to me. I know some supporters were surprised that I was chosen."

Frank recalls an unhappy start to his career at Plainmoor: "I had a terrible baptism. We lost our first game of the 1965/66 season 4-1 at Bradford City. When I arrived, some habits needed changing." He said the turning point in

United's season was the signing of West Ham's John Bond: "He came half way through the season and was a big influence in the team. He had dropped from the First Division to the Fourth to join us. In fact I was able to attract several other quality players down. They were impressed with the progressive, efficient way in which the club was run. With so many good players, it was not all that surprising we won promotion in my first year. We were a Fourth Division club with First Division players."

Frank also pinpoints another player who contributed to United's success that year: "Our goalkeeper, Terry Adlington, broke his finger so we obviously needed a replacement. Then, Gary McGuire wrote to me offering his services. He played for an amateur club in London, so I brought him down for a trial and signed him. It was a stroke of luck really. The other player who helped us tremendously in our promotion year was Tommy Spratt, who scored many of our goals. He was a "Busby Babe", but never got on very well with the crowd.

"We had no problem attracting big names to the club because the wage difference between the First and Fourth Divisions was not the same as it is now. I felt that with the high calibre of players we had we could make it to Division Two, but we just missed out. Then, after I left, a lot of the players were sold to Bournemouth and that was the start of the decline."

Frank returned during the 1976/77 season, and then again in the 1980/81 season. But he found many things had changed, most notably, the club's financial standing: "We were having to use part-time players because of the financial trouble. It was terrible, particularly in my last spell, when Bruce Rioch took over. Bruce had only recently been playing for Scotland, and now he was having to play alongside part-timers. I must admit I got a bit disillusioned. I didn't intend to stay for long in those two short spells, because for me, a return to managing a Fourth Division club was a step backwards. I wanted to help the club out, but with the situation as it was, I was not too unhappy when I called it a day and retired."

Frank still watches some of United's home matches, but added: "I like to watch a good game of football, but it is not my life anymore." He said the biggest disappointment in his career was being shown the door at Old Trafford after only eighteen months: "When I joined them in 1971 after my spell at Leicester, Manchester United were experiencing a difficult period. I took them to eighth in the First Division in my first season there. Losing my job at Manchester after only eighteen months upset me more than anything. I felt I had been treated badly, but these things happen in football."

His assistant, Jack Edwards took over as caretaker manager until 8 January 1969, when Scotsman Allan Brown took over. United's form ebbed and flowed that season to prove the theory of unpredictability was no myth. Yet they managed to finish a highly respectable sixth.

The season saw the first local derby between United and Plymouth Argyle since the 1957/58 season. And the first league clash at Home Park on 5 October became something of a grudge match after Argyle's manager Billy Bingham had announced, not very diplomatically: "Torquay are a lucky side."

United didn't need too much luck to throw those words back into Bingham's face though as United proved a point by winning 2-1. Bingham's comments that United would win the return fixture at Plainmoor on Boxing Day "over my dead body" prompted some United fans to construct a coffin for him! As it happened,the game was postponed because of a waterlogged pitch and Argyle eventually won the re-scheduled game in February 1-0.

Torquay introduced a Player of the Year vote among fans for the first time that year — and it was won by goal-keeper Andy Donnelly.

Then at the end of the season, the club suffered a major set-back when Robin Stubbs was sold to Bristol Rovers for £12,000. Stubbs now recalls one of the reasons behind the move: "I was part of a big clear-out which took place when Allan Brown took over. I was one of quite a few who left around that time." His was a severe loss to United, who could not find an adequate replacement — and in fact, they never have since.

United slid·into mid-table mediocrity for the next two years and the 1969/70 season was the scene of two major humiliations. The first came when United were knocked out of the FA Cup by non-league Tamworth and the second was delivered courtesy of Plymouth Argyle, who hammered the Gulls 6-0 at Home Park.

The year 1970 marked the arrival of local lad Ian Twitchin, who had represented England at youth level — he remained in the side for the next eleven years. The year also saw the departure of Jimmy Dunne, who was sold to Fulham for the then large sum of £17,000. He later played for Eire. Meanwhile goalkeeper Mike Mahoney made his debut for United, where he stayed for four years before being sold to North East footballing giants Newcastle. To complete the major comings and goings, Fred Binney was sold to Exeter City, a decision which back-fired as Binney proved lethal in front of goal for City.

The following year, the 1970/71 season, will be remembered for three completely different reasons.

United made a little bit of local history that season by achieving their first — and last — double over Plymouth Argyle, by winning both matches 2-1. The year saw another first when, on 17 March 1971, United's league match with Shrewsbury had to be abandoned after sixty three minutes with the score standing at 1-1 because the Plainmoor pitch resembled a lake following hours of torrential rain. United won the re-scheduled fixture 1-0.

The year will also be remembered for United's FA Cup run, which led to the most remarkable come-back ever staged by the club. United had just shocked 28,000 spectators at Villa Park by beating Aston Villa in the league when, as fate would have it, the two teams were drawn together in the Cup — this time the game would be held at Plainmoor.

United again ran out winners, this time by three goals to one. One of their goals came from ex-Villa player Dick Edwards, who celebrated scoring against his old club by doing hand-flips all the way back to the centre-circle!

After beating non-league Chelmsford 1-0 away, United were granted a home tie against Fourth Division Lincoln in the third round. It turned out to be one of the most extra-ordinary games ever to be played in the history of the FA Cup — the match had everything, and more.

The slow, over-cautious start gave no hint of what was to follow as Lincoln stunned the 8,000 crowd by romping to a 3-0 lead within the first half an hour.Their first came after seventeen minutes of tentative play, when a Micky Cave blunder let in Percy Freeman to open the scoring. 0-1. Lincoln then appeared to kill off the game with two goals in a minute. And it was Freeman again who ended a sweeping move out of defence by thumping the ball past Andy Donnelly. 0-2.

Less than sixty seconds later Phil Hubbard ran half the length of the pitch to slide the ball past the by-now bemused Donnelly. 0-3.

It was then that fate stepped in to unwittingly help United. Full-back Bob Glozier limped off after forty minutes to be replaced by Chris Barnard, who had been out for a month with a broken wrist. It proved to be the turning point of the match as United embarked on a miraculous come-back. Within a minute Cave hit one of his unstoppable "specials" from twenty five yards past Lincoln goal-keeper John McInally. 1-3.

United then looked like scoring every time they went forward — but they still looked highly vulnerable at the back. They took the second step in their remarkable recovery a minute before half-time, when John Rudge scored from the penalty spot. 2-3.

It set the second half up perfectly — and eleven minutes after the break, United were level. Barnard scored his first goal for Torquay since signing for £8,000 from Ipswich,when his diving header from an Eric Welsh cross flashed into the net. 3-3.

United were now anxious to grab the winner to avoid a replay, and constant pounding of the Lincoln goal-mouth finally paid off when Cave put Barnard through to hit his second goal of the game. 4-3.

United held on to their lead despite Lincoln's last-ditch efforts to salvage the game, although they had a few nervy moments when Lincoln first hit the bar and then the side-netting. The final whistle brought to a conclusion an astonishing ninety minutes and it meant United were through to the fourth round of the FA Cup for only the third time in their history.

They got no further however, losing 3-0 away to Leicester at Filbert Street.

4. THE DARK YEARS 1972-1986

When United defeated Chesterfield 3-2 in the first game of the 1971/72 season, there was not even the merest of hints of the disasters which were awaiting them just around the corner. Although not looking like promotion prospects, earning ten points from their first nine games, United certainly didn't look like relegation candidates either. Yet after that solid, if unspectacular, start United slumped to five consecutive draws followed by a disastrous run of eight defeats. After briefly pulling themselves together, they then lost another seven games in a row. The poor start, almost inevitably, cost manager Allan Brown his job.

On 9 October, with United cruising 2-0 up at home to Wrexham, no-one could have foreseen that the day would result in Brown having to look for another job. But United surrendered their lead woefully to eventually lose 3-2. Brown's words after the fateful match proved sadly prophetic: "This team will get me the sack. They have sold the club up the river with that performance tonight."

Two days later he was dismissed — less than three years after his arrival at Plainmoor. During his time in charge, United had received £100,000 in transfer fees — but they had lost several good players and, significantly, gates were drastically down.

Jack Edwards took over as manager, but with United's poor form, he must have known that his was a precarious position. Almost the first thing he did was to pay a club record £15,000 for Leicester City striker David Tearse. But not even he could help as United went through an appalling time in front of goal, failing to score in seven successive games after the turn of the year. United did not achieve their first victory of 1972 until 11 March, when they won 2-1 at Wrexham.

United's season was brought to life in the League Cup when, after accounting for Newport County and Oldham Athletic, they were given a plum draw at home to Spurs.

In front of 20,100 spectators, United went on all-out attack. And it came as no real surprise when they took a deserved lead through Bruce Stuckey, who gloriously smashed the ball past a helpless Pat Jennings. With the crowd dreaming of an upset, local lad Ian Twitchin undid all the good work by needlessly bringing down Martin Chivers in the penalty area when the ball was going harmlessly out of play. Martin Peters duly converted the resultant penalty. That proved to be the turning point and Spurs eventually ran out comfortable winners, 4-1.

The mini-cup run apart, the year was a disaster for United. They had not finished bottom of any division since their very first year in the Football League, and they were determined not to do so this time. They avoided that ignominy thanks to their 1-1 draw against Bolton Wanderers on the last day of the season. It was enough to lift them above Bradford City on goal average, but it was none the less small consolation for United, who were plunged into the Fourth Division — where they have remained ever since.

United's position at the end of the 1971/72 season:

Mansfield	36 pts
Barnsley	36 pts
Torquay	32 pts
Bradford	32 pts

United were well adrift of the teams above them and it would have required an almost faultless run-in to pull them out of the mire. As it happened, they lost four of their last six games.

The consequences of the 1971/72 season were felt in two ways. The most obvious one was financial, with gates plummeting in unison with United's fortunes. The second result was that now the club was in the basement division, they had greater difficulty attracting quality players to Plainmoor. Chairman Tony Boyce described the drop at the time as a "temporary set-back."

But the following year provided United with the ominous sign that getting back out of the Fourth Division would be no easy task as they finished just seventh from bottom. That season, 1972/73, was the last for Robin Stubbs, who had returned from Bristol Rovers but who was forced to retire from the game with a bad knee injury. United signed Cornishman Mike Trebilcock, who had been Everton's Cup Final hero in 1966, to take over the goalscoring role. He scored ten goals in twenty three games before being released at the end of the season.

United in fact started their first year in Division Four promisingly and were unbeaten in the first seven games. But things took a downward turn after that, which was again reflected in the lower attendances.

Eventually the club had to introduce a series of cost-cutting measures after it was reported that United were losing £1,000 a week. As part of the economies, manager Jack Edwards was sacked after spending eight years at Plainmoor in one capacity or another. In addition, the reserve team was abandoned, leaving its coach, Don Mills, out of a job. Malcolm Musgrove, who had been O'Farrell's assistant at Leicester and Manchester United, was appointed new manager.

He immediately continued the economies, retaining just thirteen professional players for the start of the 1973/74 season.

The gloom off the pitch was not lifted by United's performances on it, and they had the ineptitude of those below them to thank for keeping them out of the re-election danger-zone at the end of the 1972/73 season. United managed just forty four goals in forty six matches and ended on forty one points. Things were only marginally better the following year when United finished ninth from bottom on forty three points. Supporters were beginning to fear that United were acquiring an established look in the Fourth Division. To be fair to the management, Musgrove's hands were tied considerably by financial constraints.

United made a good start to the season, losing just two of their first thirteen games, but then slid down the table. History was made on 24 February 1974, when, because of the power crisis, United had to stage their league match with Northampton on a Sunday. The switch brought a bigger crowd, with 4,186 people turning up to watch the Gulls win 1-0.

The 1974/75 season was a case of "same again" as United ended in mid-table. If nothing else, they were getting a reputation for consistency. This time United finished on forty two points. The crisis on the pitch again spread to affairs off it, and Chairman Tony Boyce appealed to Torbay Council — and the thousands of stay-away fans — to back the club or face the real prospect of seeing it go under.

Help was on hand however from a far more distant source. Newcastle United paid Torquay a life-saving £30,000 for their outstanding goal-keeper Mike Mahoney.

United's fortunes, which were at a low ebb during the greater proportion of the seventies, saw a marked improvement in the 1975/76 season, when they lifted themselves to a much more respectable ninth position. They even managed to get out of the forties, ending the season on fifty points. The vast improvement did not prevent a number of horrific results, however, notably the 6-0 defeat at Crewe and the 7-1 thrashing at Tranmere four weeks later. Those defeats aside, fans were beginning to see some light at the end of the tunnel and awaited the next season with renewed optimism.

That optimism proved groundless though as United slipped to ninth from bottom in the year that saw Workington go out of the Football League after finishing bottom for the second year running — something United were to do themselves a few years later. Thankfully, the other clubs looked more kindly on Torquay.

Former United player Jimmy Dunne returned to Plainmoor for the 1976/77 season to add a touch of class to the side, something which was also provided by centre-half Phil Sandercock — one of the few good things to happen to the club in the seventies.

United's poor league record had already put Musgrove under a certain amount of pressure, but when the unthinkable happened and United were knocked out of the FA Cup by a non-league club, that proved to be the final nail in his coffin. Musgrove got his marching orders after United lost 2-1 at home to Hillingdon Borough in the first round.

Chairman Tony Boyce decided that drastic action was required to put a stop to United's decline in fortunes, and he turned again to Frank O'Farrell — eight years after he had left Plainmoor to pursue his globe-trotting career at Leicester, Manchester United, Cardiff City and, for a spell, in charge of the Iranian national team. He made it clear however that he would only stay on as a temporary measure until the club found someone to take over permanently.

O'Farrell must have wondered what on earth he had let himself in for when he took his place in the dug-out for the start of the United v. Cambridge league match in January 1977. United's centre-half Pat Kruse chose that game to make history, although the record for scoring the fastest ever own-goal is probably one he does not relish holding. Cambridge kicked off and immediately walloped the ball hopefully into the United half. Kruse intercepted the ball and aimed a soft back-header towards goalkeeper Terry Lee, who had unfortunately vacated his goal-mouth. Even more unfortunately he then slipped over and could only lie on his belly and watch the ball bobble into the empty net. The entire pantomime had taken just *seven* seconds from kick-off!

If that was not bad enough for perfectionist O'Farrell, even worse was to follow later in the game. As if to prove that the earlier own-goal was no fluke, United put the ball in their own net a second time just before half-time. This time it was a stupendous header by Phil Sandercock, which flew into the back of the net.

United's blushes were saved by a Willie Brown double-strike in the second half. It provided them with a vital point which lifted them to safety. Three clubs who finished below United that season have all since gone out of the league — Workington, Southport and Newport.

O'Farrell was replaced in March by centre-half Mike Green who took over as player-manager.

Local striker Colin Lee joined Torquay from Bristol City for the latter half of the season and he marked his debut by scoring — something which became rather a habit. He ended the season with ten goals from twenty three games.

League newcomers Wimbledon visited Plainmoor for United's first home game of the 1977/78 season on 27 August — exactly fifty years to the day that United had made their league debut against Exeter City in 1927 — and the result was the same, 1-1.

Two months after the start of the season Colin Lee was sold to Tottenham for a United club record of £60,000. Lee scored four goals in a dream debut as Spurs thrashed Bristol Rovers 9-0 in a televised match at White Hart Lane.

Meanwhile Mike Green led an improved United to ninth position in the league. Fourth Division champions that year were Watford, who were just starting their march all the way to Division One.

United wallowed in mid-table between 1978 and 1984 — but it was activities off the field which made most of the headlines during that period.

The 1978/79 season provided sad evidence that United were beginning to be left behind by the new breed of go-getting clubs. If the previous year had belonged to Watford, this one belonged to the upstarts of Wimbledon. The Wombles thrashed United in both league fixtures that year, winning 6-1 at Plainmoor and 5-0 at Plough Lane.

United paid a then record £25,000 for Exeter City goal-keeper Vince O'Keefe for the 1979/80 season, but the signing proved scant consolation for United fans, who mourned the sale of the club's best 'keeper since Mike Mahoney, John Turner, to Chesterfield for £40,000.

The most surprising but welcome statistic of the year however was United's goal tally. After a dearth spanning more years than many fans could care to remember, United scored seventy goals in the league, thanks mainly to the front partnership of Steve Cooper and Les Lawrence.

An indifferent 1980/81 season culminated in the inevitable with the sacking of manager Mike Green. Green was dismissed at the end of the season when they finished an undistinguished eighth from bottom. He was replaced, almost as inevitably by Frank O'Farrell. Less predictably, the former Scotland captain Bruce Rioch, who had been signed by Green on a non-contract basis, was appointed player-coach. Rioch, articulate and always a gentleman off the pitch, was an asset to the club.

United fans, fed on mediocre football for so long, could hardly believe what they were witnessing at the start of the 1981/82 season, when United romped to six wins in their first seven matches.

Rioch had brought former West Bromwich Albion striker Tony Brown to Plainmoor, and although obviously in the twilight of his career, he was the club's leading scorer that year, albeit with just eleven goals. United's tendency towards inconsistency eventually put paid to their early promotion hopes and they again finished the season nearer the bottom of the table than the top.

Rioch was made manager during the summer of 1982 and Frank O'Farrell departed from Plainmoor for the third, and, it would seem, the last time.

Rioch started by making wholesale changes in the playing staff in an effort to assemble a squad of players capable of getting United out of the Fourth Division. One of the players he brought to Plainmoor was Colin Anderson, and it was an alleged incident between the two men eighteen months later that would lead to Rioch resigning.

Amazingly, United found themselves on top of the league for a short while in the 1982/83 season. Unfortunately it was at the start rather than at the end of the season. United faded somewhat after their barnstorming start and ended the year in mid-table. Further signs of their improvement came in the FA Cup, when United reached the fourth round for only the fourth time in their history. Having beaten Colchester United, non-league Carshalton, and Oxford United, United were drawn at home to Sheffield Wednesday. The two teams played out one of the ties of the round, and Wednesday eventually

Colin Anderson showing off his Player of the Year Trophy in May 1983. An alleged altercation with manager Bruce Rioch (in January 1984) led to Rioch resigning.

ran out winners in a 3-2 thriller.

The most bizarre game of the year was reserved for the visit of Hartlepool. United won 3-2, but the game will be remembered for the fact that Hartlepool ended the game with just eight players! Already having had one player sent off, two more, Smith and Johnson, had a difference of opinion and started throwing lumps of mud at each other. Referee David Letts stunned everyone, the protagonists included, by sending the pair off.

United had a dreadful start to the 1983/84 season, with their defence letting in goals left, right and centre. They lost two of their first six matches 5-0. Torquay United was then hit by a scandal which made the front pages of the national tabloids. Rioch was alleged to have been involved in an altercation with Anderson. When the story broke in February 1984, Rioch, ever the gentleman, decided to resign to save the club further embarrassment. It was a severe blow to United for Rioch, although at the start of his managerial career, was just beginning to turn the club's fortunes around.

United could not have found a more contrasting character to replace him than his successor, Dave Webb. The colourful Cockney was still involved in a wrangle with his former club Bournemouth over alleged unfair dismissal when he arrived at Plainmoor in February. He immediately drafted in a number of his Bournemouth players, including Derek Dawkins, and Kenny Allen. He also enticed a couple of former internationals to Plainmoor — Tony Currie and Eddie Kelly. United finished the season in ninth position, having used an astonishing thirty six players in their forty six league fixtures.

The saddest statistic however occurred on May 2nd, when only 967 spectators turned up to Plainmoor to watch United beat Chester 1-0 in a league match.

Dave Webb on his arrival in February 1984 – before things turned sour. United Chairman, Lew Pope, however, claims Webb saved the club from financial ruin.

Lew Pope had by now taken over as Chairman, replacing Tony Boyce. Mr Boyce had seen United through a torrid time. In the latter years of his chairmanship, the club had asked Torbay Council for financial help. Although United lease the ground off the Council, they then owned the stands. To provide some much needed cash, the Council agreed to buy the stands off the club. It prompted some councillors to suggest the name of the club be changed to Torbay United — a suggestion which was laughed out of court.

The first thing Mr Pope, the new chairman, did was to bring Dave Webb

Torquay United 1985/86. (L to R) Back row: Paul Viner, Martin Lambert, Alan Savage, Mark Crowe, Kevin Smith, Tommy Whealdon, Vince Shearer, Simon Malim, Dave Smith, Chris Myers. Middle row: Mark Loram, Paul Compton, Steve Wright, Johnny Durham, Tony Fowler, Kenny Allen, Derek Dawkins, Peter Dearlove, Darren Cann, Steve Pugh. Front row: Mick Perry, Derek Fowler, Eddie Kelly (player coach), David Webb (Manager), Brian Wilson (Assistant Manager), John Sims, Mario Walsh.

to Plainmoor. Webb marked his first full season in charge of the Gulls by taking them to the bottom of the league. It meant, disastrously, that United had to apply for re-election for the first time since their very first season in the Football League. Thankfully, United's league record through the years was enough to convince the League's AGM that they deserved another chance and they were duly re-elected.

United had in fact finished rock bottom by a very long way — they were six points adrift of the club above them, Northampton. Their goals tally came to just thirty six and their highest scorer was Mario Walsh with a mere five goals. One good thing did come out of an otherwise dreadful season; it was the year that Brixham teenager Mark Loram made his debut — and he immediately displayed some of the natural ability which has since made him one of the best players ever to come out of South Devon.

Then, just when it seemed as if nothing else could possibly happen to United, their quite awful year was rounded off by a fire which destroyed a third of Plainmoor's fifty year old main stand. Thankfully, it broke out at about 2.30 in the morning, so there was no repeat of the tragedy which occurred at Bradford City just six days earlier, when fifty two fans perished in a stand fire during a league match.

The police at first suspected that it might have been a copy-cat arson attack, but the blaze, on 17 May, was later put down to an electrical fault. It happened just hours after fire inspectors had checked the ground. Lew Pope described the set-back as "devastating", while Dave Webb was quick to say: "Insurance does not come into it", adding that the blaze had come at a diabolical time for the club.

When the stand was rebuilt and other changes were made to the ground, Plainmoor's capacity was slashed to 4,999. It meant Torquay United did not require a Fire Certificate, something which had become compulsory for sports stadia holding more than 5,000 people after the Bradford City disaster.

During the summer of 1985, Webb announced he intended to concentrate on his job as United's first ever managing director. So he handed the job of team manager over to Stuart Morgan, who had played for the club during the sixties. The year turned out equally as disastrous as the previous one, with United finishing bottom of the league for the second year running. This time, they had even less points — thirty seven — and managed just nine wins all season while losing twenty seven and letting in eighty eight goals in the process. The omens were not good for United. Workington had been thrown out of the league just nine years earlier for finishing bottom two years running. But the other league clubs, not to mention the gods, looked more kindly on United and decided to give them one last chance.

A surprising piece of news that year surrounded the club's financial situation, which was in much better shape than expected. United's Annual

General Meeting revealed profits of £77,000.

Webb left Plainmoor at the end of the 1985/86 season — to the relief of many United followers, but not of the Chairman, Lew Pope. Mr Pope feels Webb has been much maligned since his departure: "The criticisms levelled at him have been very unfair. In many ways, he saved the club financially," said Mr Pope, somewhat cryptically.

Webb himself has readily admitted that he made mistakes during his spell at Plainmoor, but maintains that they were committed, to some extent, because of the problems which already existed at the club before his arrival: "I faced a lot of problems when I arrived and I tried to sort things out."

His departure closed an unhappy chapter in United's history. Never before had they finished bottom of the league in successive years. And they soon realised what a close shave they had had when the Football League announced that in future, the club finishing bottom would be automatically relegated to the Vauxhall Conference League.

United's position at the end of the 1985/86 season:

Preston NE   43 pts
Torquay   37 pts

5. 1987 – The Great Escape

None of the 3,493 people who witnessed the drama and emotion inside Plainmoor on the last day of the season on Saturday, 9 May 1987, will ever forget it. Yet none of them will ever want to endure the like of it again either!

It is hard to believe that a game of football can leave grown men in tears — but many were after United's 2-2 draw with Crewe Alexandra. United, after 4,140 minutes of league football that season, were on the brink of non-league oblivion, bottom of the Football League and looking over a precipice which led to the Vauxhall Conference League. But in a breath-taking finale, they saved themselves in the very last minute of the very last game of the season to pull off the escape to end all escapes.

United found themselves on the last day of the season knowing that only a win would definitely lead them to safety after yet another disastrous league campaign. This was the first year of the automatic relegation rule — there would be no turning back this time if United finished bottom for the third year in a row.

They started the season without their most talented player after selling Mark Loram to Queens Park Rangers. Mark made a return to Plainmoor later in the year after failing to settle in the capital. There were no signs of impending doom at the start of the season when United lost only two of their first eight games.

But it all started to go wrong when they were hit by a run of six successive defeats during October and November. They recovered briefly to put together a string of consistent results — but the warning bells had already been rung.

The visit of Wolves and, more to the point, their followers, was to lead the club, on the advice of the local police, to introduce an identity card system. The Wolves supporters invaded the pitch during the match in November and caused trouble in Torquay town centre during the day. Those disturbances brought to an end United's policy of Saturday night kick-offs which had been a feature for so many years — and which had always attracted bigger crowds.

Meanwhile, United's league position was becoming increasingly precarious as the end of the season grew nearer, and it was becoming ever clearer that they would have to win a good number of their last ten games to pull themselves clear of the danger zone.

Also looking perilous were Rochdale, Tranmere, Stockport, Hartlepool and Burnley. The latter had captured the nation's imagination as nobody wanted such a great old club to drop out of the league — except the followers of the other doom-threatened clubs. Hardly anyone considered Lincoln City, who had spent most of the season in mid-table, to be in any danger.

Disastrously, United won just three out of nine before the final game against Crewe — and it left them odds-on favourites to become the first

The Torquay United squad at the start of the 1986/7 season. (L to R) Back row: Darren Cann, Chris Myers, Trevor Webber, Dale Wreford. Middle row: Les Chappell (trainer), Mario Walsh, John Impey, Gerry Nardiello, John Smeulders, Phil King, Martin Ellicott, Mark Crowe, Paul Compton, Jim McNichol, Alan Morris (physio). Frontrow: Derek Dawkins, Steve Phillips, Gary Richards, Stuart Morgan, Paul Dobson,

49

A smoke bomb is thrown and Wolves fans spill onto the pitch during a disturbance at the United v. Wolves league game in November 1986.

victims of the new relegation rules. Stuart Morgan was down to the bare bones of his small squad in the second half of the season and was forced to introduce a number of inexperienced youngsters. It also meant Derek Dawkins had to play with a broken wrist in United's 2-2 draw at Burnley in April because Morgan simply did not have a replacement.

United suffered a major setback in their fight for league survival just five days before the Crewe game. They desperately needed at least a point from their difficult match at high-riding Orient. And they seemed to have achieved that, with the score standing at 2-2 after ninety minutes. Then United were dealt a blow when Orient's right back Terry Howard marked the occasion by scoring his first ever goal to send the Gulls crashing 3-2.

So United's future rested on the last day of the season. The candidates for the drop had now been whittled down to three — Burnley, who were at home to Orient, Lincoln, who were away to Swansea, and Torquay. United at least had the comfort of knowing their destiny lay in their own hands. They had forty seven points. Burnley only had forty six and were bottom of the league. Lincoln had forty eight and seemed in least danger.

Many fans who turned up on 9 May had not been to Plainmoor for years and were anxious to cheer on United in what might, conceivably, be their last

Stuart Morgan

ever game in the Football League. And that's what it looked like being after just forty three minutes when Crewe, who had obviously not come as sacrificial lambs, appeared to have condemned Torquay by taking a 2-0 lead. What made it worse for United fans was that the second goal by David Platt was clearly yards offside — again proving that when you're down, nothing goes right.

United's Jim McNichol doesn't mind admitting now that at that point, he thought it was all over bar the shouting: "When the two goals went in in the space of five minutes, I thought that was it. Half-time in the dressing room was terrible. We just said to ourselves that we had to try our hardest. What we had to get was a quick goal after the break."

And they did — courtesy of McNichol himself. His twenty-yard free-kick

The moment United were saved — Paul Dobson turns and hits the last ditch equaliser against Crewe in May 1987. Watching anxiously for United are Jim McNichol, Tom Kelly and Alan McLoughlin.

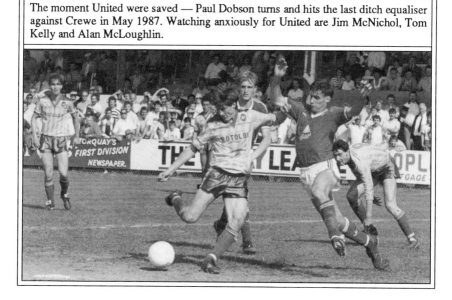

51

was deflected into the Crewe net just two minutes into the second half to set up the most nail-biting finale anyone in the ground could care to remember. Crewe, after outplaying United in the first half, were hanging on for dear life in the second. Adie Mann hit the bar for United as they went on all-out attack for the goal which might just save them. Yet despite attack after attack, the ball simply refused to go in.

Then, seven minutes from time, of all the unlikely things, a police dog intervened. Bryn the Alsatian will always go down in Plainmoor folklore as the saviour of Torquay United. Bryn, much to the chagrin of his handler, PC John Harris, sunk his teeth into McNichol's groin as the right-back thumped the ball up the wing. It took four minutes to patch up the wound — and it was in the fourth minute of injury-time added on by referee Howard King that United got their life-saving equaliser.

While the repair work was being carried out to McNichol's leg, Morgan shouted to his players that Burnley were winning: "We need a draw — we need a goal," he yelled at them.

And, gloriously, they got it with virtually the last kick of the game, of the season. United had Crewe defender Terry Milligan to thank initially for

No hard feelings — Jim McNichol shakes Bryn's paw after the Crewe game.

getting in a pickle in his own penalty area. Paul Dobson didn't need a second invitation. Grabbing the lifeline that was being thrown to him and his side, he pounced and hit the ball on the turn past Brian Parkin in the Crewe goal. It sneaked into the far corner of the net by an inch — but it was enough.

Delirium broke out, even though many in the crowd still did not know if a draw would be sufficient. But McNichol knew: "Someone had told me Lincoln were losing at Swansea so I knew we only needed a draw during the second half. Even then, it seemed for quite a while that it wasn't going to be our day."

United played out the tense dying seconds. Before Dobson's goal, they wanted the game to go on all afternoon. Now they were screaming for the final whistle, and the relief etched on the players' faces when Mr King duly obliged was there for all to see.

As for the dog-bite, McNichol joked later: "As a defender, I'm usually more worried about dodgy tackles from forwards, not a police dog. It's the most bizarre thing that has ever happened to me in football. You certainly don't expect to be attacked by a police dog on the pitch. But there were no hard feelings. Bryn must have seen me out of the corner of his eye and thought I was going for him or his handler. It hurt like hell, but it gave us the extra minutes to score, so I was delighted."

McNichol, who needed seventeen stitches, admitted he couldn't stand up after the incident and if it had been any other game, he would have come off.

Dobson, somewhat unluckily over-shadowed by Bryn, was the real hero of the hour — and he revealed afterwards that he had foreseen what would happen: "I had this premonition I would score the goal that kept us up and I never gave up hope."

An emotionally drained Stuart Morgan, who was mobbed by hundreds of ecstatic fans at the final whistle, summed it all up succinctly when he said: "I always said it would go to the last game of the season, but the last minute of the last game is something else. Before, in the previous games, there was always a feeling of, well, there's still the next game. But for the Crewe game, there would be no tomorrow. We had to do it then. It got to the younger players — they were petrified."

For Chairman Lew Pope, a United fan for nearly sixty years, the final whistle spelt doom: "I thought we were out of the league. I didn't realise Lincoln had lost. In fifty five years of watching Torquay, I have never seen scenes like it." After the game, Mr Pope expressed what every Gulls fan had gone through during the previous nine months: "It's been a terrible strain all season. I never want to go through that again."

So it was poor old Lincoln City who went down — but only because their goal difference was marginally worse than United's. It was the first time that they found themselves bottom of the league that season — but they had

Stuart Morgan and Lew Pope after United's 2-2 draw with Crewe Alexandra in May 1987.

chosen the only time that it counts. They had, in fact, beaten United 1-0 in the league fixture at Plainmoor in October, while the return game in March ended in a 1-1 draw.

The Lincoln story had a happy ending though as they returned to the Football League a year later after winning the Vauxhall Conference League at the first attempt.

After the post-Crewe euphoria had died down, the United Chairman had another battle on his hands — to keep Morgan at Plainmoor. Morgan was keen to stay but feared he was not entirely wanted. He had also become increasingly frustrated at the lack of cash available to buy much-needed new players. "I was determined to keep United in the league no matter what. But I've got a feeling it hasn't always been appreciated in some quarters," was how Morgan summed up his feelings after the Crewe game.

It soon became clear to him that his future lay elsewhere and, during the summer, he left for non-league Weymouth before eventually moving along the south coast to Bournemouth as youth development officer.

Morgan's departure was a loss to Torquay — he knew a good player when he saw one and was always a believer in good, skillful football. He left the club with the best squad of players in years, something which his successor, Cyril Knowles, was able to capitalise on.

How the bottom of Division Four looked come 4.46 pm, on Saturday, 9 May:

	P	F	A	Pts	
Burnley	46	53	74	49	
Torquay	46	56	72	48	-16
Lincoln	46	45	65	48	-20

The team that saved United: Kenny Allen, Jim McNichol, Dave Cole, Derek Dawkins, Tom Kelly, Chris Myers, Alan McLoughlin, Mark Gardiner, Mario Walsh, Paul Dobson, Mark Loram, and substitute Adie Mann.

With contributions from: Bryn, Terry Milligan, Swansea City FC, and referee Howard King, who added on four minutes of injury time.

6. PROMOTION HEART-ACHE 1987/88

After the near-disaster of the previous year, Cyril Knowles was installed as United's new manager for the start of the 1987/88 season, with Chairman Lew Pope hoping he could bring about a major transformation in the club's fortunes.

Having finished bottom of the league two years running and then next to bottom on goal difference the following season, United fans could have been forgiven for expecting another nine months of agonising football.

Knowles relied mainly on the players left behind by Stuart Morgan — players like Tom Kelly, Jim McNichol, and Dave Cole. In fact, it could be argued that United's best side for years was inherited by Knowles but actually assembled by Morgan.

Knowles made a change to the style of play, though, using three central defenders in a five-man defence. That allowed United's full-backs, McNichol and Kelly to push forward and help out in attack.

Bearing in mind what had gone before, most Gulls fans were left rubbing their eyes in disbelief on the first day of the season, as United hammered Wrexham 6-1 at a sweltering Plainmoor. After going 1-0 down, United then took complete control, with Paul Dobson helping himself to a hat-trick. Knowles modestly put the win down to the heat, saying the folk in Wrexham were not as accustomed to the heat as their Torquay counterparts!

Knowles himself could never have anticipated such an astonishing start to the season. The fans certainly hadn't — only 1,731 turned up to watch the game. The result did, however, raise a few eye-brows, as did their next result, a 1-0 win at Colchester.

So it was that an extra thousand fans attended the next match at Plainmoor, in which United earned a 1-1 draw against a strong Orient side.

United lost just three of their first thirteen league fixtures — a record which justifiably established them as early promotion hopefuls. And when they continued their impressive form to lose just one out of ten matches immediately after Christmas, it eventually dawned on the Torbay public that Division Three football the following season was a realistic possibility.

Attendances rocketed to 3,500, which had been unheard of in the previous years, when under 2,000 was the norm. Wins at home to Carlisle United and away at Halifax in the penultimate week of the season set United up for what looked like almost certain promotion. But disaster struck in the last week of the season, when they lost 1-0 at Burnley and 2-1 at home to another promotion-chasing side, Scunthorpe United. A win in either of those last two matches would have sent United up to Division Three, which they had vacated sixteen years earlier.

The Burnley game proved a nightmare for the usually dependable leftback, Tom Kelly. It was his ill-judged back-pass to Kenny Allen which led to

Burnley's winner. Despite dominating much of the game, United could not find the back of the net, and were left to rely on winning the last, nerve-wracking game of the season.

A capacity crowd of just under 5,000 stood in disbelief as Scunthorpe, who out-played United for much of the game, won the match 2-1, with United's goal coming from Paul Dobson. It was sweet revenge for Scunthorpe, who had lost the earlier fixture with United that season by three goals to two.

United's away form was a revelation right throughout the season, winning eleven league games away from Plainmoor. Scunthorpe's surprise win meant that they had clinched a play-off spot. It also meant that United had missed out on automatic promotion. Their fall at the last hurdle meant they now had to face the drama of the play-offs. United fans were by now accustomed to biting their nails — it was getting to be something of a May-time ritual.

As fate would have it, United were pitched against Scunthorpe in the first round of the play-offs — and the two-legged tie brought out all the tension that had simmered just below the surface during their encounter the week before.

The first leg was played at Plainmoor on Sunday, 13 May in front of 4,602 fans who, despite their optimism, still had a lingering feeling United may have missed the boat. Those feelings were soon dispelled as the Gulls took a two-goal lead in the first forty five minutes. The first came from a Dave Caldwell header and the second from the ever-reliable boot of Dobson.

The do-or-die nature of the game got the better of the Scunthorpe side, who, after United's goals, proceeded to fall apart. Referee Tony Ward booked six players and sent off Scunthorpe's Paul Nichol as tempers flared.

Just as United looked set to take a two goal advantage to Scunthorpe for the second leg, veteran goalkeeper Kenny Allen handed the visitors a gift of a goal, dropping the ball for Andy Flounders to score.

Despite all the action on the pitch, it was manager Cyril Knowles who made the headlines. He left his dug-out after a heated discussion with the referee. Knowles was angry at a foul committed on Caldwell — and told the referee so. At first it was thought Knowles had been sent off, but he explained afterwards he had walked off voluntarily in case he said something which would warrant the red card.

The two sides re-convened three days later and a Mark Loram goal was enough to secure a 1-1 draw in front of 6,500 spectators. So United had won 3-2 on aggregate, putting them through to the last stage of the play-offs, which was to be against Swansea City.

The Welsh side really had no right to be in with a chance of promotion — they had only managed to finish sixth in the league — but such were the anomalies of the new system.

United's draw would have suited most teams. It meant the first leg of the tie would be played at the Vetch and the second at Plainmoor. But it didn't suit United, whose strength all season had been to grab a lead and defend it. Knowles would have preferred United to play at home first, get their noses in front, and stay there.

As it was, United lost the game at the Vetch 2-1, with McNichol scoring for the Gulls. The defeat came as something of a shock as Torquay's away form that year had been a revelation. And in fact the result did not do United justice as they had been on top for much of the match. United did at least have the return game in which to turn the tide and snatch promotion.

Cyril Knowles

The encounter, played throughout in driving rain, will go down as one of the most exciting games played at Plainmoor. A capacity crowd of 5,000 expectant fans rolled in to witness what most of them hoped would be an historic day for Torquay United. This would be the day when they would finally make it out of the Fourth Division — not downwards, as many had anticipated at the season's outset, but, almost miraculously, upwards. The ban on away supporters was lifted for the game, as indeed it had been for the previous tie with Scunthorpe.

United were left shell-shocked after just twenty minutes, when Swansea held a two-goal lead and seemed to have killed off the game once and for all. It meant they were 4-1 up on aggregate and it appeared that United's dreams of playing Third Division football for the first time since 1972 had been shattered.

After the two goals, Knowles immediately sent on teenage winger Lee Sharpe, who was playing his last game for Torquay before joining Manchester United. And it was his cross that sparked off a come-back, with United scoring twice in five minutes to pull level on the day. Jim McNichol headed Sharpe's cross into the net to make it 1-2, and it was the right back who again found the back of the Welsh net just five minutes later.

But then, right on the stroke of half-time, Swansea regained the initiative when Alan Davies scored their third, and decisive goal.

The second half was all United, with every player bar Torquay 'keeper Kenny Allen camped in the Swansea half for much of the forty five minutes.

The pressure paid off in the sixty sixth minute when Dave Caldwell headed in to make it 3-3.

With away goals counting double in the event of a tie, however, United knew that, despite being only 5-4 down on aggregate, they would still need two more goals to get through. They in fact could have scored a hatful, but none of the endless stream of chances would go in.

So it was Swansea who were promoted to Division Three and United who were to play the following season in the Fourth Division for the sixteenth consecutive year. Yet none of the United fans who were at Plainmoor on 28 May are likely to forget one of the most pulsating ninety minutes many of them had ever seen. Nor will they quickly forget the sight of United's dejected players having to be led from what was now a bog of a pitch, some of them in tears.

It was just twelve months earlier that United were in a do-or-die situation of a very different kind. Some felt Knowles' big mistake was leaving Sharpe

One of Plainmoor's most popular players in recent years, Derek 'The Dude' Dawkins is carried shoulder-high off the pitch after scoring the winner against Spurs in the first leg of the second round Littlewoods Cup tie at Torquay in September 1987.

on the substitutes' bench. It was after his introduction that things started to happen for Torquay — and it was he who created their first two goals. Afterwards, Knowles criticised the play-off system, but one of his experienced players, Derek Dawkins added: "Football is not about what might have been. It's about taking your chances and we had enough but didn't take them. At the end of the day, the rest doesn't matter."

Such realism was little consolation for United, who stayed down after finishing fifth while Swansea, who finished sixth, went up. But United had once again caught the imagination of the Torbay public, which was no mean achievement, the resort being more of a tennis hotbed in recent years than a football one.

Quite apart from their heroic league endeavours, United also grabbed the national headlines on two other occasions that season — for an historic win over Spurs, and over the sale of sixteen-year-old Lee Sharpe to Old Trafford.

Having accounted for Swansea in the first round of the Littlewoods Cup, formerly the League Cup, United were rewarded with a plum draw against Tottenham in the second. The first leg took place at Plainmoor on 24 September, when a capacity crowd of 4,999 (although it looked more like 10,000) turned up half expecting an upset.

Spurs, boasting internationals Ray Clemence, Ossie Ardiles, Chris Waddle, Steve Hodge et al., were none the less considered suspect under pressure away from White Hart Lane. And so it proved for, after a good opening spell from the North London club during which Kenny Allen pulled off a string of desperate saves, United proceeded to take control.

The game was heading for a 0-0 draw though with just three minutes left, when the crowd's favourite, Derek 'The Dude' Dawkins ghosted into the Spurs penalty area to blast the ball past a helpless Clemence. United survived some close calls in the little time which remained to take their 1-0 lead into the second leg.

With United in irrepressible form, particularly away from home, thousands of Gulls fans headed for London a fortnight later with justifiable optimism. Knowles was back on familiar territory of course, having spent his playing days at White Hart Lane.

United, who had to avoid conceding an early goal at all costs, were dealt a blow in only the fourth minute, when Belgian international striker Nico Claesen gave Spurs the lead, hooking the ball into United's net from two yards.

But United then fought back and Spurs had Clemence to thank for two stunning saves to foil Dobson and McNichol. The crowd of 20,970 were just beginning to entertain thoughts of another upset when the unfortunate Dave Cole headed a low, hard cross past his own goalkeeper ten minutes before half-time to give Spurs a flattering 2-0 lead.

United knew that one goal would win them the tie on the away goals rule and attacked Tottenham throughout the second half. But the luck was with the Londoners and they kept out United's forwards before Claesen killed off the tie nine minutes from time with his second (and Spurs' third) goal of the game.

The season was one of what might have beens and after the Spurs game, Cyril Knowles said: "With a bit of luck it could have been much different, but we certainly did ourselves proud." Those sentiments were to be echoed

Lee Sharpe, shortly before leaving for Old Trafford in May 1988.

seven months later.

United's find of the season was a lanky, skinny sixteen-year-old from the West Midlands. Lee Sharpe was brought to Plainmoor as a Youth Training Scheme apprentice after being rejected by his local club Wolves. His close skills, pace and dribbling ability on the left wing attracted scouts from several big clubs, but even he was dumbfounded when Knowles turned up at his digs at one o'clock one morning in April 1988 to tell him Manchester United manager Alex Ferguson had made a bid for him. Lee stayed with United until the end of the season and joined the Old Trafford club during the summer. The deal, after instalments, has so far brought Torquay £180,000.

Lee was immediately thrown into the Manchester side after a series of injuries decimated Ferguson's squad. He filled in at left-back for a spell before reverting to his usual position on the left flank. His performances earned him an England Under-21 cap, and in the 1989/90 season he scored his debut goal for the "Red Devils".

An incident-packed season was almost capped by a surprise Wembley appearance. United reached the southern semi-final of the Freight Rover Trophy, a competition introduced to give teams from the two lower divisions the opportunity to play at Wembley.

After beating Bristol Rovers, Hereford United, Port Vale and Aldershot, United fans were beginning to think of the impossible. But they were then pitched against the runaway leaders of the Fourth Division, Wolves, and lost 1-0 at Molineux. Wolves went on to win the final that year. Sweeping all before them in the Third Division the next year, they thought they were going to win it again — but United were, of course, to exact glorious revenge for their earlier defeat.

United also reached the third round of the FA Cup in the 1987/88 season. After knocking out non-league Bognor Regis Town and then Bristol City, United were drawn away to FA Cup holders Coventry City, where they were slightly unlucky to lose 2-0.

United ended their best season since the days of Frank O'Farrell in the 1960s with nothing concrete to show for it. They had finished the season on seventy seven points — their highest total under the three-points for a win system. They had scored sixty six league goals and conceded only forty one. They had also had three exciting cup runs.

United's success was reflected at the turnstiles, with 67,965 fans watching United's home matches during the year — an average of 2,955. And after the final game of the season, the heart-breaking play-off clash with Swansea, Gulls' fans were all eagerly awaiting the next season. After years lying dormant the club and its followers had been re-awakened by United's success — and the prospect of more to come.

7. UNITED'S FINEST HOUR

If the Gulls' exploits the year before had brought a temporary halt to the spate of Torquay United jokes, then what transpired in 1989 put an end to them once and for all.

Cyril Knowles' main aim for the 1988/89 season was, of course, to achieve the promotion United had only narrowly missed out on the previous year. They got off to an inauspicious start however, losing their first two games of the season to start off cries of "Here we go again."

They recovered to win the next three matches, only to lose the following one at Scarborough 5-2. United were, in fact, the epitome of inconsistency and the league season, from start to finish, was one of complete unpredictability. It is what makes supporting Torquay so much more interesting than following almost any other football team in the country. It was evident that the loss of striker Paul Dobson to Doncaster Rovers during the summer had provided a void no other forward at Plainmoor could fill, and his goals were sorely missed. It was equally apparent that United's away form, which was so impressive the year before, had deserted them.

Any hopes United had of sneaking into a promotion play-off spot were smashed in a run of three successive defeats in April — the last of which was a humiliating 4-0 drubbing at the hands of neighbours Exeter City at Plainmoor. The league programme ended in a whimper with just 2,066 turning up to watch United lose 3-1 at home to Colchester United, who were relegated to the Vauxhall Conference League at the end of last season.

With United struggling to get their league act together, they turned to the cup competitions to provide them with success. If United's league campaign was noticeable for their lack of consistency and dearth of away victories, then the story was the exact reverse in their cup performances. They reached the third round of the FA Cup after knocking out non-league clubs Fareham and Yeovil, both ties going to replays. The third round draw paired them with Sheffield Wednesday, who were then stranded at the bottom of the First Division. Needless to say, in keeping with tradition, United were drawn away. Pundits immediately picked out the tie as one ripe for an upset. And so it appeared when Dean Edwards gave United an early lead.

But, as they say, United had scored too early, and it only served to wake Wednesday up. The match was the turning point of their season as they went on to beat United 5-1, a scoreline which flattered them. It seemed United would have to wait another year before making an impression on the Wembley trail....

Meanwhile, United were progressing very nicely in the strangely entitled Sherpa Van Trophy. United lost 1-0 at Swansea in the first game of the preliminary round, which meant they had to win their next match at home to Cardiff to progress to the first round proper. A paltry 1,187 turned up to see them do just that, winning comfortably 3-1 on a cold December night. That obviously caught the imagination of the Torquay public — a little. 1,884 attended the next tie at home to Third Division Gillingham. United completely outplayed their supposed superiors, beating them 3-0. That pitched them against another Third Division side, Bristol Rovers. But this time United did not have the advantage of playing at Plainmoor. Not many gave them an earthly, but a Mark Loram curling 'special' from twenty yards gave them a surprise 1-0 win.

Fans were now beginning to sit up and take notice — although United still had to overcome yet another Third Division side away from home in the Southern semi-final. If anything, Brentford posed a bigger obstacle to United's Twin Tower dreams than Rovers had. Thousands sat beside their radios, knowing that if only United could get through this one, they would be just one tie away from Wembley. Centre-half Phil Lloyd answered their prayers, scoring the only goal of the game to stun 5,802 Londoners.

Torquay's cup form had been such that they did not fear their Southern Final opponents, Wolves, who were leaders of the Third Division. The West Midlands club had accounted for United in the competition twelve months before. More relevantly, they had also swept all before them in the Third Division, with the fearsome striking partnership of Steve Bull and Andy Mutch scoring at will all season.

The first leg was played at Plainmoor on Wednesday, 12 April, and while nobody else was giving United a chance, they and their fans quietly anticipated an upset.

Those expectations seemed justified as a capacity crowd watched United completely outplay Wolves and take a deserved lead through Dean Edwards. A Mark Loram corner from the right was headed back across the area by Matthew Elliott and Edwards, a former Wolves player, was on hand to nod the ball in. That same combination was to be in evidence at Wembley a month later.

So United went in a goal up at half-time, but Wolves could have had no complaints if the scoreline had been trebled, with Jim McNichol having a good-looking goal disallowed and Ian Weston hitting the post during the first forty five minutes.

It was again all one-way traffic in the direction of the Wolves goal in the second half, but United failed to convert any of their chances. Then, with just four minutes left, disaster struck — twice. The prolific Bull, who had not been allowed a sniff of the ball all night, scored two stunning goals to seemingly bring an end to Torquay's Wembley dreams. United justifiably felt they had been robbed and immediately set about working out how on earth they could secure a 2-0 victory at Molineux — something no other team had done all season.

Dean Edwards after scoring United's goal against Wolves at Plainmoor in the first leg of the Sherpa Van southern final in April 1989.

No amount of optimistic talk from Knowles could convince anyone that Wolves would be in for a shock when the two sides met again six days later. The omens were not good — United had lost their previous two league games 3-1, but that did not deter 400 United hopefuls travelling up to the Black Country to witness an unbelievable ninety minutes — and one of the biggest football shocks of the season.

Wolves attacked from the start, but could not find an opening through United's five-man defence. Then the 22,532 supporters, with the exception of 400 of them, were stunned into silence when United broke and scored after only eight minutes. A beautiful through-ball from Loram let in Edwards, who controlled the ball before hitting a low eighteen yard shot into the corner of the net.

After scoring so early, United knew they were in with a chance, but they also knew they had to get another.

Wolves meanwhile roared into attack — but again all their chances went a-begging. And they were left in tatters two minutes before the interval when United caught them napping. Loram took a twenty five-yard free-kick before

Wolves' goal-keeper Roger Hansbury had time to adjust his wall. The perfectly placed curling shot went around the wall, past the flailing arms of Hansbury and into the top corner of the net. The half-time scoreline left everybody, United fans included, in a state of shock. If the result remained the same, United would be at Wembley and the holders would be out. But it was a big if.

What followed was the most nerve-wracking forty five minutes most Gulls fans could remember. At least in the second half of the Crewe game two years earlier United were 2-0 down and most sane fans had all but given up hope. In a perverse way, being ahead made it all the more nail-biting.

Wolves pushed forward straight after the interval, looking for the goal which would put their noses in front again. But when Bull incredibly missed a sitter after just three minutes, the United contingent in the crowd started to believe this was to be their night. Bull and Mutch, who had scored sixty six goals between them that season, could not find a way through United's rock-solid defence.

Torquay goalkeeper Kenny Allen, who had been brought out of retirement by Knowles following an injury to Ken Veysey, pulled off a miraculous save, tipping a Keith Downing shot over the bar when it had 'goal' written all over it.

The last five minutes seemed an eternity with Wolves piling on attack after attack. But United somehow managed to keep them out, and they made history when referee Brian Hill blew the final whistle. It was the first time any Devon football club had reached a Wembley final. After the game Chairman Lew Pope described it as the "greatest night of my life," while Knowles modestly put the win down to his players.

Yet in reality it was tactical decision to have his defenders stand off the two Wolves' strikers that stifled the most feared strike-force in the football league. He discovered that Bull and Mutch preferred defenders to push up and mark them tightly — because that enabled them to beat the offside trap. "The important thing was to prevent them getting behind us — and it worked," said Knowles.

Wolves were left sick as the proverbial parrot. But Bull was later to get ample compensation for the defeat. The day before the Sherpa Van Trophy Final, he made his scoring debut for England against Scotland at Hampden Park. Thus Torquay United were to a large extent responsible for him embarking on his international career — if Wolves had reached the final as expected, Bully would not have been available to play for England.

Meanwhile, United's unlikely heroes started preparing for the day none of them could have imagined in their wildest dreams. That applied particularly to 37-year old Kenny Allen, who had been released from Plainmoor on a free transfer by Knowles at the end of the previous season.

Cyril Knowles meets guest of honour Elton John before the Sherpa Van Final.

And 20,000 South Devon folk, some of whom had never been to a football match before in their lives, started their preparations for, of all the unlikely things, a Wembley cup final.

Their opponents on a gloriously sunny day on Sunday, 28 May, were Bolton Wanderers, who had reached the final after a controversial Northern final tie against Blackpool. Another Third Division side, they were immediately installed as favourites, while United were again considered rank outsiders.

But 20,000 yellow-clad Devonians had by now decided that Torquay's name was written on the cup and that United were about to lift the first trophy in their history.

United took the opportunity to rid themselves of the unpopular all-white

strip and introduce the nostalgic yellow kit.

When skipper Jim McNichol led the team onto the famous Wembley turf, United fans could have been forgiven for thinking it was all a fanciful dream — but the day was not to have a dream ending, as Torquay's footballing fairy-tale ended in tears.

If the luck had been with them against Wolves, it sadly deserted them at Wembley. Yet for four all too brief minutes, United were ahead. The first twenty three minutes of the game were nip-and-tuck, with nothing to choose between the two sides. Then United earned a corner on the right at the tunnel end of the stadium. Loram's cross was headed backwards at the near post by Elliott and Edwards nodded the ball into the gaping net. It was a carbon copy of the goal against Wolves at Plainmoor.

United's fans were at the other end of the stadium and not many of them could claim to have seen much of the goal, but it didn't stop them going wild — United were 1-0 in a Wembley cup final! All cameras were focused on the giant electric scoreboard as thousands snapped up the moment for posterity.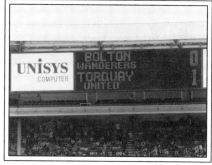

Edwards meanwhile couldn't contain himself and sprinted all the way to the United bench for a well-deserved hug.

The celebrations had hardly died down when Bolton were level. United failed to clear a corner and Julian Darby turned and shot past Kenny Allen from sixteen yards. That was the cue for Bolton to put United under sustained pressure for the first time in the match, but United held on until halftime.

After the interval it was United's turn to go on the attack, and their Third Division opponents were forced into a spell of desperate defending. But then came the turning point. After sixty three minutes, Lady Luck smiled on the Lancastrians. It was difficult to see at that point how Bolton were ever going to score — barring a fluke. And that was precisely what happened. Breaking out of defence, Bolton's Jeff Chandler crossed the ball into United's penalty area more out of hope than anything else. With no danger in sight, United's man of the match, John Morrison stuck out a boot, only to see the ball fly into the net past a helpless Allen. United's players sank to their knees at the injustice of it all.

To their credit, they got back up again and pounded the Bolton goalkeeper Dave Felgate with a wave of attacks. Felgate pulled off crucial saves from Daral Pugh, Mark Loram and Dean Edwards. But United, by necessity, were now leaving gaps at the back — which a skillful Bolton side were able to

exploit by scoring two goals in two minutes. Dean Crombie broke out of defence to finish a sweeping move after seventy nine minutes to make it 3-1 and Trevor Morgan completed the scoring by adding a fourth after eighty one minutes.

No-one in the crowd of 46,513 could deny Bolton were the more cultured side, but the scoreline flattered them, and more. They had luck to thank for giving them the lead and Felgate for keeping them there.

United's players and fans were reluctant to leave the stadium, despite the defeat, and afterwards Knowles stressed to his despondent players that they should not let the result ruin the greatest day of their careers. "It was a great day, and I just told them to enjoy it," said Knowles.

Goalscorer Dean Edwards said the biggest disappointment was not holding on to their lead for longer, and added: "The goal was typical of many we've scored this season. Scoring at Wembley gave me a wonderful feeling, but we didn't have time to celebrate."

Top left: Goal! Dean Edwards puts United ahead.
Bottom left: Edwards starts his sprint to the United bench after scoring. Also pictured is Carl Airey (in front of Jim McNichol) and Matthew Elliott.
This page: Mark Loram ready to pounce, but Bolton's Dave Felgate held on.

69

The saddest man on the pitch at the end of the game was teenager John Morrison, whose deflected own-goal swung the game Bolton's way. But he was cheered up by ever-the-humourist Kenny Allen, who said: "I didn't want the game to end, and then I thought 'hang on, it could end up 8-1!'."

Club chairman Lew Pope summed up the incredulity felt by everyone that Torquay had even reached a Wembley final in the first place when he said: "To think, two years earlier we were nearly out of the league! The final showed just how much the club means to the town."

The game was to be Jim McNichol's last game for United — and he rates 28 May 1989 as the pinnacle of his career: "Leading Torquay United out at Wembley is the highlight of my career. It's got to be. The whole day was wonderful—the build-up, the crowd, everything. The biggest disappointment was not hanging on to our lead for longer, and although they were the better side, the scoreline flattered them."

McNichol rates his three years at Plainmoor as the most eventful period in his playing career: "They will always go down as the three 'nearly' years. We nearly went out of the league, nearly won promotion and then we nearly won a cup."

The Wembley line up:

Torquay United:		Bolton Wanderers:	
1.	Kenny Allen	1.	Dave Felgate
2.	Daral Pugh	2.	Phil Brown
3.	Tom Kelly	3.	Barry Cowdrill
4.	Jim McNichol	4.	Robbie Savage
5.	Matthew Elliott	5.	Dean Crombie
6.	Mark Loram	6.	Mark Winstanley
7.	Carl Airey	7.	Jeff Chandler
8.	Phil Lloyd	8.	Steve Thompson
9.	Dean Edwards	9.	John Thomas
10.	Ian Weston	10.	Trevor Morgan
11.	John Morrison	11.	Julian Darby
12.	Jimmy Smith	12.	Stuart Storer
13.	Sean Joyce	13.	Ian Stevens

Torquay United made two substitutions during the match: Jimmy Smith replaced Carl Airey after seventy one minutes and Sean Joyce came on for Ian Weston after seventy three minutes. Bolton's Jeff Chandler was replaced by Stuart Storer after eighty minutes.

Torquay United's "Road to Wembley".

Round	Date	Opponents	Score	Scorers	Att.
Preliminary	28.11.88	Swansea (A)	0-1	-	1,409
Preliminary	2.12.88	Cardiff (H)	3-1	Roger Gibbins (2), Jimmy Smith	1,187
First	17.1.89	Gillingham (H)	3-0	Daral Pugh (pen), Sean Joyce, Jimmy Smith	1,844
Quarter-Final (S)	22.2.89	Bristol R (A)	1-0	Mark Loram	4,316
Semi-Final (S)	21.3.89	Brentford (A)	1-0	Phil Lloyd	5,802
Final, first leg (S)	12.4.89	Wolves (H)	1-2	Dean Edwards	4,612
Final, second leg (S)	18.4.89	Wolves (A)	2-0	Dean Edwards, Mark Loram	22,532

8. CHANGES

Many changes have, of course, taken place at Torquay United during the seventy years since they turned professional in 1921.

The most frequent changes relate to the playing strip. During the 1920s, United played in black and white striped shirts and white shorts — that led to them being nick-named The Magpies, a name which lasted right up until the 1960s.

After the war, United's new kit of white shirts and black shorts became established. That was replaced under manager Eric Webber in the 1950s by a new strip which was introduced to reflect Torquay's image of sun, sand and sea. Thus United played in gold shirts and blue shorts until that was finally dispensed with in the seventies.

In came the anaemic-looking all-white strip, with two blue stripes sandwiching a yellow stripe down the right side of the shirt in the 1975/76 season.

Hot on the heels of that came the new look of white shirts and blue shorts with a dash of yellow down the side. There were, in fact, several quite unnecessary changes to the kit during the 1970s, none of which were popular and none of which lasted longer than a season.

Bruce Rioch, showing he had style off the pitch as well as on it, insisted on the re-introduction of a predominantly yellow and blue strip when he arrived at Plainmoor.

Then came Dave Webb ... he immediately felt it was about time Torquay United were given the Chelsea look and, during the mid-eighties, they were condemned to play in all blue. Not a very popular move that — no wonder crowds plunged to under a thousand — watching their beloved United dressed up like Chelsea was much more than many fans could stomach.

Then came the return of the anaemic all-white, and quite dreadful it looked too.

Finally came the all-yellow, which was introduced for the Wembley cup final in May 1989. And, in a move prompted by nostalgia, United's away strip became the same as their original first-team strip back in those early days in the twenties — black and white striped shirts and white shorts.

Although United had long since dispensed with their striped kit, they remained known as The Magpies right up until the sixties when, in keeping with the sun, sea and sand theme, they were re-named The Gulls.

Not surprisingly therefore, United got a new club logo, although the last twenty five years or so has seen a variety of seagulls displayed on the team's shirts. The traditional club crest, although still on show at the Plainmoor ground, is now nowhere to be seen on the playing kit.

Changes to the ground were kept to a minimum until the advent of Dave Webb. The wooden grandstand, in place since 1927, remained more or less intact until the fire of 1985. The terracing remained the same as well until, under Webb, the two sections on either side of the ministand and the standing area at the Babbacombe end were all flattened. That led, necessarily, to a drastic reduction in the ground capacity. Having coped with crowds of over 20,000, Plainmoor's capacity was decimated to just 4,999. It was raised back to 6,000 prior to United's FA Cup third round tie with West Ham United in the 1989/90 season.

Dave Webb also masterminded the change of use to the mini-stand, which had always been used by the younger, more noisy element of Torquay's followers. It was made an all-seater family stand — five years before all football league clubs were told to rid their grounds completely of terracing.

United became one of the first clubs in the lower divisions to introduce floodlights — that was during the 1954/55 season. The original lights were then replaced on 23 December 1960 by a new set of floodlights which cost the club £9,000.

The changing rooms and manager's office have been re-located in recent years. They were moved from the grandstand side of the ground to behind the family stand at the Ellacombe end. The players have fared somewhat better than the manager from the switch — the manager's office comprises a 'temporary' porta-cabin.

One of Torquay United's trademarks during the sixties, seventies and the greater part of the eighties was their policy of playing their matches on Friday, and then Saturday nights. It proved popular with the South Devon public, who turned up in larger numbers than for afternoon kick-offs. The policy had to be changed following the visit of Wolves in November 1986, when some of their supporters caused trouble in Torquay town centre during the afternoon before the game. South Devon's police chiefs advised the club to switch their kick-off times to Saturday afternoons to prevent a repeat of the incidents in future.

The pitch invasion by Wolves fans that night was also the main reason behind the introduction of identity cards, which every United fan needs to get into the ground. There was even a temporary ban on all away fans for a while! But new Chairman Mike Bateson has, in the 1990/91 season reintroduced Friday night games and amended the membership card scheme.

Even the pitch itself has not escaped from the odd alteration or two. Most recently, the pitch was narrowed by a yard on the instructions of manager Cyril Knowles, who felt the change would suit his tactics better.

Considering that seventy years have passed since 1921, changes at Torquay United have been surprisingly few and far between, primarily because of financial constraints. Following the Hillsborough disaster of 1989 however, Plainmoor will have to be transformed in the next ten years.

9. CHARACTERS

Every football club throws up it characters — and Torquay United has proved to be no exception. The various peculiarities and bizarre goings-on of the last few years in particular has resulted in the birth of Plainmoor legends of a different kind — bell-ringer John Bartlett and Bryn the police dog to name but two.

But there are other, lower profile characters who have played a part behind the scenes at Plainmoor. One, Freddie King, was responsible for keeping the Plainmoor turf in ship-shape condition to handle the pounding of nearly a thousand league and cup games. He took over as groundsman in 1951 and retired thirty six years later in 1987. During that time he got to know every nuance of the Plainmoor pitch — and observed the ups and downs of United's performances on it.

After watching more United matches than most, Freddie is well placed to evaluate the teams through the years. And it was the side of the early and mid-fifties which he rates as the best he has seen: "The team that we had when I started was in my opinion, the best we have ever had. The players of that decade were also the best we ever had. Sammy Collins, our greatest goal-scorer, Ronnie Shaw, our best winger, and Don Mills, who was the best player ever to play for us.

"The Third Division South was a much stronger league than the present Fourth Division — it was very nearly as good as the Second Division is now.

"The league system then was better than it is now. There is far too much travelling involved these days. We always had players that people wanted to pay to see — like Robin Stubbs during the sixties. But football has changed since those days and there are not so many personalities around."

Not least of those changes is the width of the Plainmoor playing surface, which Freddie was asked to alter by Cyril Knowles: "I had to narrow the pitch to fit in with his tactics. I could understand why Knowles wanted it narrowed because it suited his style of play, which concentrated more down the centre of the pitch than down the wings. But I think it would pay now to have that extra yard of width back."

Dealing with the likes and dislikes of the various Plainmoor managers became second nature to Freddie, who outstayed all of them: "I worked with so many managers during the years, and they were all different but my job was to do what they wanted as far as the pitch was concerned."

He categorically refuses to comment, however, on the Dave Webb era — a period, he says, he would rather forget about.

Not many football clubs can claim to have had a Nashville singing duo in their ranks — but Torquay United can. Dick Edwards and Bruce Stuckey made a name for themselves by singing Country and Western music around pubs and clubs. And they rounded off their musical career by visiting the centre of C&W — Nashville, USA. Former Aston Villa player Edwards even made a record, a tuneful little ditty entitled 'Oh United', which had a distinctive early seventies feel to it. The world of Country and Western was never the same after the duo decided to hang up their guitars.

On a more serious note, United, under Cyril Knowles, acquired for themselves a vital member of the England World Cup squad. Physiotherapist Norman Medhurst made a surprise decision to leave Chelsea and move down to South Devon. He first discussed the move with England manager Bobby Robson, who assured him it would not jeopardise his position in the England set-up. Thus Norman decided to leave the city life for the relative calm of Torquay. Norman became England physio sixteen years ago and has been to three World Cup Finals — a far cry from Plainmoor. Yet he says he has found very little difference between the two set ups: "As far as I'm concerned they are all professional footballers and the injuries are the same. So my job is very much the same whether I'm with England or Torquay.

"Neither is there any difference between the two sets of players when it comes to physical fitness. The thing which sets them apart is that international players have the mental awareness. They see things more quickly, and, without wishing to sound derogatory, they use their heads more than the average Fourth Division player."

One difference he has found dealing with the players at United is that they tend to be more receptive to what he has to say: "They are not under the same sort of pressure so they are easier to get through to. Players right at the top are entertainers and are under more pressure, so they tend to get more up-tight. With them, you are not only dealing with their injuries, you are dealing with their personalities as well."

Norman himself rarely gets up-tight and is not a nervous watcher: "I'm usually cool and calm throughout the game, but I feel drained afterwards. But I take life as it comes. If we win, we win, and if we lose, it's not worth crying over spilt milk. You have to be philosophical if you are involved in sport."

The experience of 1988/89, however, when United were at one stage lingering perilously close to the bottom of the league was a kind of pressure Norman had not had to deal with before: "Being threatened with going out of the league was something I'd never had to handle before and it was a relief when when we were safe," said the physio.

10. 1989/90

After the euphoria of a glorious, unexpected Wembley cup final appearance, Cyril Knowles shocked the Plainmoor faithful by putting virtually the entire squad on the transfer list.

United's wages bill of £6,000 a week had to be pruned, but Knowles' reaction did appear somewhat drastic. The biggest disappointment for United fans came when club captain Jim McNichol joined rivals Exeter City on a free transfer after failing to agree a new contract with Knowles. The Wembley game proved to be McNichol's last for the Gulls, although he admits he didn't want to leave Plainmoor: "I never wanted to leave. I was always very happy at Torquay and wanted to stay."

He left to join his old club, Exeter, who had themselves released him three years earlier because they said he could not run his Ashburton pub and play league football at the same time. How wrong they were!

Centre-half Dave Cole was also allowed a free transfer to Rochdale while, in another example of generosity, Tom Kelly was allowed to join York City free of charge. He has since, of course, joined up with McNichol at Exeter.

The transfers followed a similar decimation of the squad the previous year when Knowles released Kenny Allen, Mark Gardiner, Derek Dawkins, and John Impey, among others.

Mark Loram meanwhile was diagnosed as a diabetic, but decided he was fit enough to continue his footballing career.

After the previous three eventful years, it seemed there was little else that could happen to United — and fans eagerly anticipated another year of success.

But after a disastrous start, which included six defeats in a row, Knowles resigned. It had been obvious for some time that he and Lew Pope did not always see eye to eye. Knowles had recently been pictured in the local papers allegedly tearing up his contract, although it later turned out to be a piece of paper symbolising his contract. He was unhappy at Mr Pope revealing that he had received a payment of £16,000 from the Wembley profits. The apparent bad feeling between the two men culminated in Knowles leaving Plainmoor at the end of September, to be replaced a few days later by former Plymouth Argyle manager Dave Smith. The glory of just four months earlier had turned horribly sour.

In United's ninety three league games under Knowles, they had won thirty eight, drawn twenty two, and lost thirty three. They scored 107 goals in those games, and conceded 102. In twenty six cup games, they had won fourteen, drawn three and lost nine. Knowles may not always have been the best public relations man in the world, but nobody could argue with his record at Plainmoor.

United were languishing at next to bottom of the league when Knowles departed, and already had the spectre of 1987 looming large before them. Thankfully, they then started to get their act together and a string of good results at home lifted them clear of the danger-zone, although it was touch and go right up until March.

The year was punctuated by a whole series of incidents, the most bizarre of which occurred during the home game with Maidstone, making their Plainmoor debut in their inaugural year in the league, on 30 December. Torquay's former town crier, John Bartlett, an ardent United follower for forty years, inadvertently sparked off a near-riot by, of all things, ringing his bell.

When the police received a complaint from two supporters and a linesman, they moved in and asked him to stop ringing the bell, which had become his trademark in recent years. That was the cue for scores of fans to run to his assistance and general bedlam ensued. The result of the incident was a ban until the end of the season for Mr Bartlett, who had previously been featured on the front cover of United's match day programmes.

It prompted him to announce: "I've been ringing my bell up here for fifteen years — and I'm not going to stop now. The ban is diabolical. If you can't ring a bell at a football match, then there's something seriously wrong. Everyone used to bring rattles to matches in the old days, and that was allowed."

The club countered that the match officials had reported United to the Football League over the incident and the ban was a measure to preempt any action they might take. As it happened, no action was taken.

The ban meant Mr Bartlett missed the Plainmoor match the following week, when United met West Ham in the third round of the FA Cup. The Hammers, newly relegated to the Second Division were, none the less, still

Paul Hirons celebrates his winning goal against West Ham Utd.

firm favourites to advance to the fourth round — despite the furore surrounding their then manager Lou Macari.

But they hadn't reckoned with eighteen-year-old Paul Hirons grabbing his first ever goal with his very first touch of the match after coming on as substitute. The match proved to be the highlight of an otherwise poor season for United — and United's winning goal came courtesy of a fluke.

With the game ebbing and flowing from one end of the pitch to the other, United broke out of defence through winger Paul Smith. His cross was met by Robbie Taylor, who miscued his shot, sending the ball horizontally across the West Ham penalty area straight to Hirons, who placed the ball past the despairing Phil Parkes. Hirons had only been on the park for three minutes!

It meant United had reached the fourth round of the Cup for the first time since the 1982/83 season, and for only the fifth time in their history. But they failed to reach the fifth round for the first time ever, losing 1-0 at Blackpool.

The year saw an extra-ordinary row break out between United and neighbours Exeter City over the newly entitled Leyland Daf competition, known as the Sherpa Van Trophy the year before when, of course, United reached the final. United, having drawn at home with Bristol Rovers and lost at Exeter, relied on City doing them a favour by beating Rovers by three clear goals in the final game of the round-robin stage. City left out several of their key players for the match, which Rovers duly won 3-0.

An incensed Torquay immediately reported City to the Football Association, claiming they had broken the rules by not playing their strongest available side. The FA's resultant enquiry cleared City, who explained the multiple absenteeism was due more to injuries than a ploy to rest players for their up-coming league fixture. The FA decided they were telling the truth and the matter rested there.

As if all that excitement wasn't enough, the weather even had a say in the 1989/90 proceedings. United's home game with Gillingham in November had to be called off an hour before the kick-off when a sixty-foot tree crashed down on terracing on the popular side. With other trees threatening to follow in the 100 mph winds, it was decided the game could not go ahead for safety reasons. If the tree had been blown down an hour later, there would have been a disaster. That was later followed by more storm damage, this time in January, when half of the main grandstand roof was blown away.

A wind-fall of a very different kind befell United that season, however. Phil King, whom United had sold to Swindon Town a couple of seasons earlier, received somewhere in the region of £130,000 when the Wiltshire club sold him to First Division Sheffield Wednesday, or at least they were a First Division club when they bought him! United, as part of the deal which took King to Swindon, were entitled to a third of the transfer fee — and Wednesday paid £400,000 for him.

The 1989/90 season was also a record-equalling year, with Sammy Collins' long-standing record of scoring in seven consecutive league matches finally being matched by Carl Airey in the game against Carlisle United at Plainmoor in November. He in fact could have beaten the record, which was set during the 1954/55 season. The following match, United were awarded a penalty in the third minute of the re-scheduled fixture with Gillingham. But Mark Loram stepped up to take it — and missed!

United ended a somewhat disappointing season in the bottom half of the Fourth Division. Just two weeks after the last game of the season, Chairman Lew Pope stood down and was replaced by local self-made millionaire Mike Bateson, the founder of a double-glazing firm.

Thus it brought to an end five quite astonishing years in which United successfully sought re-election to the league two years running, escaped going out of the league by scoring in the last minute of the last game of the next season, narrowly missed out on promotion to the Third Division, and finally, reached a Wembley cup final. They have also caused upsets in cup competitions, beating West Ham and Spurs against the odds. What other football club can claim to have had more ups and downs in that short period?

Incidents off the pitch came equally thick and fast. One manager departed amidst allegations of an altercation with one of his players, another became the club's first ever Managing Director, while yet another was photographed tearing up a piece of paper symbolising his contract. A drastic cut in Plainmoor's capacity; a fire burning down the main stand; storms blowing away the roof on that same grandstand — all these incidents have ensured that Torquay United has rarely been out of the news in the last five years.

The last few years have brought with them such bizarre incidents as Bryn the police dog attacking Jim McNichol, a former town crier being banned for ringing his bell, and a ball-boy calmly walking onto the pitch to take the ball off the feet of an opposing player advancing towards United's goal (surely such incidents can *only* happen at United) — it all adds up to the most eventful period in the club's history.

11. THE FUTURE

Bearing in mind Torquay United's rather turbulent history, it would be a brave person who would predict how the next seventy years will shape up. One thing is certain however: every club in the Fourth Division will be casting a watchful eye over their shoulder as long as the present automatic relegation system is in force. United, like all the others in the basement league, face the potential of non-league obscurity every single season. But it does provide an added impetus, as if it was needed, to get out of the danger area by way of promotion to the Third Division. After 1987, we can only hope it is something United never have to worry about again.

Quite apart from the playing side of things, the next decade promises to be one of the busiest in United's history. After the Hillsborough disaster and the resulting Taylor Report, Plainmoor will *have* to be made all-seater by the year 2,000. New Chairman Mike Bateson has said improvements will be made to the ground in the coming years, with plans for new stands being made.

Mr Bateson, who now has a controlling fifty one percent of Torquay United, has already invested a quarter of a million pounds into the club. He said his number one aim is to make United a self-sufficient club: "We are still broke, so changes are needed. Three years ago, the club was broke to the brink of extinction. We had an overdraft of £350,000. That has now been brought down to a reasonable level. We live hand to mouth, but we are in a better position than many Fourth Division clubs.

"We will be staying at Plainmoor in the near future, but a move to a new ground is a possibility in the longer term. It will need peripheral activities to make the club self-sufficient. We can't do that at Plainmoor, so from that point of view, we will need to move. There are no plans for that yet though. The main priority is to make Torquay United more high profile. We need more fans through the turnstiles and we need to get back into the Third Division. I see no reason why we shouldn't."

Certainly, United seemed to have ushered in a bright new future under their new, go-getting Chairman. United's weekly wages bill was recently quoted to be about £6,000, with profits from home games coming to only £3,000 or so — hence Mr Bateson's desire to attract more spectators into Plainmoor. United's massive overdraft of three years ago has been brought down thanks to the Wembley appearance and the sales of Lee Sharpe and Phil King. Mr Bateson has recently introduced a share flotation to raise cash for the club, with supporters able to buy shares in the club at £1.00 each.

One possible change in the offing in the near future could well be a return to the old North/South divide league system. The topic has been raised several times in the past by the league's ninety two clubs, but the move for the switch back has gained momentum of late.

Certainly, travel-wise, a return to Football League Division Three (South) would make a lot of sense for United, who do more hiking up and down the country than virtually every other club — much to the discomfiture and cost of both club and supporters.

Financially, it would benefit United but, on the minus side, it would mean the end of visits to Plainmoor by great old clubs such as Burnley and Blackpool.

It is a topic dealt with hilariously by United's club fanzine *Mission Impossible*, which described the ordeal of being a travelling Gulls fan thus:

> Away Travel with Torquay United — all Matches Except Hereford, Exeter and Orient:
>
> From Gordano Services, travel upwards until you reach an urban sprawl where they used to make cars. Keep going until you run out of motorway and it becomes a bit more hilly and colder. Ask directions from there. Do not be scared by the fearsome looking Northerners with their flat caps and clogs — they are really quite friendly. Set off early so as to leave time for lunch — traditional black pudding, chips and gravy. A word of warning however — water sterilisation tablets and hygiene jabs are recommended. Sun lotion need not be carried.

Which just about sums up what United fans have to endure for the privilege of watching their team.

Whatever happens in the years to come, Torquay United has out-lived many other clubs who could not stand the pace, even if things did get a wee bit touch and go for a while during the mid-eighties. But they got through those little hiccups and now the club's centenary year awaits just around the corner — in 1999.

It all began in earnest in 1899, when Torquay United Association Football Club was first formed on an amateur basis. Things got a little more serious of course in 1921, when the club turned professional and reverted back to its original name after a brief flirtation with the title of Torquay Town. The seventy years since then has provided an enormous amount of fun. Here's to the centenary ... and beyond that, the next seventy years!

League Record since joining the Southern League in 1922

		P	W	D	L	F	A	Pts	Pos
1922/3	Southern	38	18	8	12	63	38	44	6th
1923/4	Southern	34	19	7	8	59	25	45	4th
1924/5	Southern	38	9	11	18	41	73	29	15th
1925/6	Southern	26	12	5	9	59	46	29	6th
1926/7	Southern	26	17	4	5	63	30	38	1st
1927/8	Div 3(S)	42	8	14	20	53	103	30	22nd
1928/9	Div 3(S)	42	14	6	22	66	84	34	18th
1929/30	Div 3(S)	42	10	11	21	64	94	31	19th
1930/1	Div 3(S)	42	17	9	16	80	84	43	11th
1931/2	Div 3(S)	42	12	9	21	72	106	33	19th
1932/3	Div 3(S)	42	16	12	14	72	67	44	10th
1933/4	Div 3(S)	42	13	7	22	53	93	33	20th
1934/5	Div 3(S)	42	18	6	18	81	75	42	10th
1935/6	Div 3(S)	42	16	9	17	62	62	41	10th
1936/7	Div 3(S)	42	11	10	21	57	80	32	20th
1937/8	Div 3(S)	42	9	12	21	38	73	30	20th
1938/9	Div 3(S)	42	14	9	19	54	70	37	19th
1946/7	Div 3(S)	42	15	12	15	52	61	42	11th
1947/8	Div 3(S)	42	11	13	18	63	62	35	18th
1948/9	Div 3(S)	42	17	11	14	65	70	45	9th
1949/50	Div 3(S)	42	19	10	13	66	63	48	5th
1950/1	Div 3(S)	46	14	9	23	64	81	37	20th
1951/2	Div 3(S)	46	17	10	19	86	98	44	11th
1952/3	Div 3(S)	46	18	9	19	87	88	45	12th
1953/4	Div 3(S)	46	17	12	17	81	88	46	13th
1954/5	Div 3(S)	46	18	12	16	82	82	48	8th
1955/6	Div 3(S)	46	20	12	14	86	63	52	5th
1956/7	Div 3(S)	46	24	11	11	89	64	59	2nd
1957/8	Div 3(S)	46	11	13	22	49	74	35	21st
1958/9	Div 4	46	16	12	18	78	77	44	12th
1959/60	Div 4	46	26	8	12	84	58	60	3rd
1960/1	Div 3	46	14	17	15	75	83	45	12th
1961/2	Div 3	46	15	6	25	76	100	36	21st
1962/3	Div 4	46	20	16	10	75	56	56	6th
1963/4	Div 4	46	20	11	15	80	54	51	6th
1964/5	Div 4	46	21	7	18	70	70	49	11th
1965/6	Div 4	46	24	10	12	72	4	58	3rd
1966/7	Div 3	46	21	9	16	7	54	51	7th
1967/8	Div 3	46	21	11	14	60	56	53	4th
1968/9	Div 3	46	18	12	16	54	46	48	6th
1969/70	Div 3	46	14	17	15	62	59	45	13th
1970/1	Div 3	46	19	11	16	54	57	49	10th
1971/2	Div 3	46	10	12	24	41	69	32	23rd
1972/3	Div 4	46	12	17	17	44	47	41	18th
1973/4	Div 4	46	13	17	16	52	57	43	16th
1974/5	Div 4	46	14	14	18	46	61	42	14th
1975/6	Div 4	46	18	14	14	55	63	50	9th
1976/7	Div 4	46	17	9	20	59	67	43	16th
1977/8	Div 4	46	16	15	15	57	56	47	9th
1978/9	Div 4	46	19	8	19	58	65	46	11th
1979/80	Div 4	46	14	17	14	70	69	47	9th
1980/1	Div 4	46	18	5	23	55	53	41	17th
1981/2	Div 4	46	14	13	19	47	59	55	15th
1982/3	Div 4	46	17	7	22	56	65	58	12th
1983/4	Div 4	46	18	13	15	59	64	67	9th
1984/5	Div 4	46	9	14	23	38	63	41	24th
1985/6	Div 4	46	9	10	27	43	88	37	24th
1986/7	Div 4	46	10	18	18	56	72	48	23rd
1987/8	Div 4	46	21	14	11	66	41	77	5th
1988/9	Div 4	46	17	8	21	45	60	59	14th
1989/90	Div 4	46	15	12	19	53	66	57	15th

United's First Year in the Football League 1927/8

Aug	27	H Exeter City	D	1-1
	29	A Millwall	L	1-9
Sep	3	A Merthyr	W	3-1
	7	H Millwall	L	0-1
	10	A Norwich	L	0-4
	17	H Northampton	L	1-5
	24	A Southend	L	0-1
Oct	1	H Brighton	D	1-1
	8	A Bournemouth	D	1-1
	15	H Brentford	W	2-1
	22	H Charlton	L	1-2
	29	A Bristol Rov	L	1-5
Nov	5	H Plymouth A	L	1-2
	12	A Watford	W	2-1
	19	H QPR	W	1-0
Dec	3	H Newport	D	1-1
	10	A Walsall	L	0-4
	17	H Gillingham	D	1-1
	27	H Crystal Pal	L	0-2
	31	A Exeter	L	0-5
Jan	7	H Merthyr	D	2-2
	14	A Coventry	L	1-5
	21	H Norwich	W	4-2
	28	A Northampton	D	4-4
Feb	4	H Southend	D	3-3
	11	A Brighton	L	0-3
	18	H Bournemouth	D	2-2
	25	A Brentford	W	2-1
Mar	3	A Charlton	L	0-1
	10	H Bristol Rov	D	0-0
	14	A Crystal Pal	L	2-3
	17	A Plymouth A	L	1-4
	24	H Watford	D	1-1
	31	A QPR	W	3-2
Apr	6	A Luton	L	0-2
	7	H Coventry	L	2-3
	9	H Luton	L	0-4
	14	A Newport	D	2-2
	21	H Swindon	W	2-1
	28	A Gillingham	L	1-4
May	2	A Swindon	D	2-2
	5	H Walsall	D	1-2

Division Three South 1927/8

	P	W	D	L	F	A	Pts
Millwall	42	30	5	7	127	50	65
Northampton	42	23	9	10	102	64	55
Plymouth A	42	23	7	12	85	54	53
Brighton	42	19	10	13	81	69	48
Crystal P	42	18	12	12	79	72	48
Swindon T	42	19	9	14	90	69	47
Exeter C	42	17	12	13	70	60	46
Southend	42	20	6	16	80	64	46
Newport C	42	18	9	15	81	84	45
QPR	42	17	9	16	72	71	43
Charlton	42	15	13	14	60	70	43
Brentford	42	16	8	18	76	74	40
Luton T	42	16	7	19	94	87	39
Bournemouth	42	13	12	17	72	79	38
Watford	42	14	10	18	68	78	38
Gillingham	42	13	11	18	62	81	37
Norwich C	42	10	16	16	66	70	36
Walsall	42	12	9	21	75	101	33
Bristol Rov	42	14	4	24	67	93	32
Coventry C	42	11	9	22	67	96	31
Merthyr T	42	9	13	20	53	91	31
Torquay	42	8	14	20	53	103	30

United's League Record in 1956/7
(when they missed out on Promotion to Division Two by a Decimal Point)

Aug	18	H Ipswich T	W 2-0
	23	A Walsall	W 1-0
	25	A Bournemouth	D 0-0
	29	H Walsall	W 2-0
Sep	1	A Exeter	D 1-1
	4	A Watford	L 1-4
	8	H Millwall	W 7-2
	12	H Watford	W 3-0
	15	A Brighton	L 0-6
	17	A Shrewsbury	D 1-1
	22	H Gillingham	D 3-3
	26	H Shrewsbury	D 1-1
	29	A Swindon	W 2-1
Oct	6	H Coventry	W 3-1
	13	A Norwich	W 2-1
	20	H Colchester	W 4-2
	27	A Newport	L 0-3
Nov	3	H Reading	W 3-1
	10	A Plymouth A	D 0-0
	24	A Northampton	L 0-3
Dec	1	H Southend	D 3-3
	15	A Ipswich	L 0-6
	22	H Bournemouth	W 1-0
	25	A Brentford	D 0-0
	26	H Brentford	W 2-0
	29	H Exeter	W 1-0
Jan	12	A Millwall	L 2-7
	19	H Brighton	W 1-0
	26	A Aldershot	W 1-0
Feb	2	A Gillingham	D 1-1
	9	H Swindon	W 7-0
	16	A Coventry	L 2-3
	23	H Norwich	W 7-1
Mar	2	A Colchester	L 1-2
	9	H Crystal P	W 3-0
Mar	13	H Aldershot	W 4-2
	16	A Reading	L 1-3
	23	H Plymouth A	D 1-1
	30	A QPR	W 1-0
Apr	6	H Northampton	W 2-0
	13	A Southend	L 0-2
	19	H Southampton	W 2-0
	20	H Newport	W 4-0
	22	A Southampton	L 0-1
	27	H QPR	W 3-0
May	1	A Crystal P	D 1-1

Division Three (South) 1956/7

	P	W	D	L	F	A	Pts
Ipswich Town	46	25	9	12	101	54	59
Torquay Utd	46	24	11	11	89	64	59
Colchester	46	22	14	10	84	56	58
Southampton	46	22	10	14	76	52	54
Bournemouth	46	19	14	13	88	62	52
Brighton	46	19	14	13	86	65	52
Southend	46	18	12	16	73	65	48
Brentford	46	16	16	14	78	76	48
Shrewsbury	46	15	18	13	72	79	48
QPR	46	18	11	17	61	60	47
Watford	46	18	10	18	72	75	46
Newport	46	16	13	17	65	62	45
Reading	46	18	9	19	80	81	45
Northampton	46	18	9	19	66	73	45
Walsall	46	16	12	18	80	74	44
Coventry	46	16	12	18	74	84	44
Millwall	46	16	12	18	64	84	44
Plymouth A	46	16	11	19	68	73	43
Aldershot	46	15	12	19	79	92	42
Crystal Pal	46	11	18	17	62	75	40
Exeter City	46	12	13	21	61	79	37
Gillingham	46	12	13	21	54	85	37
Swindon T	46	15	6	25	66	96	36
Norwich C	46	8	15	23	61	94	31

United's League Record in 1959/60
(when they were promoted to Division Three under Manager Eric Webber)

Aug	22 H Doncaster R	W 2-1		
	27 A Northampton	L 0-3		
	29 A Workington	W 2-0		
Sep	2 H Northampton	W 5-3		
	5 H Rochdale	D 1-1		
	9 H Southport	W 4-0		
	12 A Gateshead	W 2-0		
	15 A Southport	W 2-1		
	19 H Darlington	L 1-2		
	21 A Stockport Co	W 1-0		
	26 A Aldershot	W 3-1		
	30 H Stockport Co	W 4-0		
Oct	3 H Barrow	W 3-2		
	7 A Gillingham	L 0-1		
	10 A Watford	W 1-0		
	17 H Oldham Ath	W 4-1		
	24 A Carlisle	L 0-2		
	31 H Notts Co	W 3-1		
Nov	7 A Walsall	L 2-3		
	21 A Crewe A	W 2-1		
	28 H Chester	L 1-2		
Dec	12 H Bradford PA	D 1-1		
	19 A Doncaster R	W 3-1		
	26 H Exeter C	L 2-3		

	28 A Exeter C	L 0-1
Jan	2 H Workington	W 2-1
	9 H Hartlepools	W 3-0
	16 A Rochdale	L 2-4
	23 H Gateshead	W 1-0
	30 A Crystal P	D 1-1
Feb	6 A Darlington	L 0-1
Feb	13 H Aldershot	W 2-1
	27 H Watford	W 2-1
Mar	5 A Oldham A	W 2-0
	12 H Carlisle	W 2-1
	19 A Notts Co	D 1-1
	26 H Walsall	W 2-1
Apr	2 A Hartlepools	L 0-4
	9 H Crewe A	W 5-2
	15 A Millwall	L 0-2
	16 A Chester	D 1-1
	18 H Millwall	D 2-2
	23 H Crystal P	W 2-1
	27 H Gillingham	W 2-0
	30 A Bradford PA	D 2-2
May	2 A Barrow	D 1-1

Division Four Table in 1959/60

	P	W	D	L	F	A	Pts
Walsall	46	28	9	9	102	60	65
Notts Co	46	26	8	12	107	69	60
Torquay	46	26	8	12	84	58	60
Watford	46	24	9	13	92	67	57
Millwall	46	18	17	11	84	61	53
Northampton	46	22	9	15	85	63	53
Gillingham	46	21	10	15	74	69	50
Crystal P	46	19	12	15	84	64	50
Exeter C	46	19	11	16	80	70	49
Stockport	46	19	11	16	58	54	49
Bradford PA	46	17	15	14	70	68	49
Rochdale	46	18	10	18	65	60	46
Aldershot	46	18	9	19	77	74	45
Crewe A	46	18	9	19	79	88	45
Darlington	46	17	9	20	63	73	43
Workington	46	14	14	18	68	60	42
Doncaster	46	16	10	20	69	76	42
Barrow	46	15	11	20	77	87	41
Carlisle	46	15	11	20	51	66	41
Chester	46	14	12	20	59	77	40
Southport	46	10	14	22	48	92	34
Gateshead	46	12	9	25	58	86	33
Oldham A	46	8	12	26	41	83	28
Hartlepools	46	10	7	29	59	109	27

United's League Record in 1961/2
(when United were relegated from the Third Division to the Fourth)

Aug	19	H	Crystal P	L	1-2		26	H	QPR	D	2-2
	22	A	Grimsby	W	3-2		30	A	QPR	L	0-6
	26	A	Bournemouth	L	1-3	Jan	6	A	Southend	L	1-2
	30	H	Grimsby	L	1-2		13	A	Watford	L	1-4
Sep	2	H	Watford	L	3-4		20	H	Hull	W	4-2
	7	H	Barnsley	W	6-2	Feb	3	A	Northampton	W	2-1
	9	A	Hull	L	0-4		10	H	Lincoln	L	3-4
	16	H	Northampton	L	1-2		17	A	Bradford PA	L	1-3
	20	H	Portsmouth	L	0-2	Feb	19	A	Halifax	L	0-1
	23	A	Lincoln	W	3-1		24	H	Coventry	W	1-0
	27	A	Portsmouth	L	0-2	Mar	3	A	Brentford	W	2-0
	30	H	Bradford PA	L	1-3		10	H	Port Vale	W	2-0
Oct	6	A	Coventry	D	2-2		17	A	Bristol C	L	1-4
	11	H	Halifax	L	2-3		24	H	Southend	D	2-2
	14	H	Brentford	W	3-1		31	A	Notts Co	L	0-2
	21	A	Port Vale	L	1-4	Apr	2	H	Peterboro	L	1-3
	28	H	Bristol C	L	1-3		7	H	Shrewsbury	W	3-1
Nov	11	H	Notts Co	D	3-3		14	A	Peterboro	L	1-2
	18	A	Shrewsbury	D	1-1		20	A	Swindon	W	1-0
Dec	2	A	Reading	L	0-1		21	H	Reading	D	0-0
	9	H	Newport	W	3-2		23	H	Swindon	W	3-0
	16	A	Crystal P	L	2-7		28	A	Newport	W	3-0
	22	H	Bournemouth	W	2-1	May	2	A	Barnsley	L	2-4

Division Three Table in 1961/2

	P	W	D	L	F	A	Pts
Portsmouth	46	27	11	8	87	47	65
Grimsby	46	28	5	12	80	56	62
Bournemouth	46	21	17	8	69	45	59
QPR	46	24	11	11	111	73	59
Peterborough	46	26	6	14	107	82	58
Bristol City	46	23	8	15	94	72	54
Reading	46	22	9	15	77	66	53
Northampton	46	20	11	15	85	57	51
Swindon T	46	17	15	14	78	71	49
Hull City	46	20	8	18	67	54	48
Bradford PA	46	20	7	19	80	78	47
Port Vale	46	17	11	18	65	58	45
Notts Co	46	17	9	20	67	74	43
Coventry C	46	16	11	19	64	71	43
Crystal Pal	46	14	14	18	83	80	42
Southend	46	13	16	17	57	69	42
Watford	46	14	13	19	63	74	41
Halifax	46	15	10	21	62	84	40
Shrewsbury	46	13	12	21	73	84	38
Barnsley	46	13	12	21	71	95	38
Torquay	46	15	6	25	76	100	36
Lincoln	46	9	17	20	57	87	35
Brentford	46	13	8	25	53	93	34
Newport Co	46	7	8	31	46	102	22

United's League Record in 1965/6
(the first under Manager Frank O'Farrell
when they won Promotion to Division Three)

Aug	21	A Bradford C	L 1-4			8 H Darlington	L 0-4
	25	H Newport Co	W 1-0			15 A Chester	D 1-1
	28	H Chesterfield	W 2-0			29 H Bradford C	W 4-3
Sep	4	A Rochdale	W 3-2	Feb	5	A Chesterfield	D 1-1
	11	H Luton T	W 2-0			12 H Wrexham	W 3-1
	13	A Newport Co	L 2-3			16 A Aldershot	L 2-3
	18	A Barrow	L 0-2			19 H Rochdale	W 4-0
	22	H Southport	D 1-1			26 A Luton T	L 2-3
	25	H Hartlepools	W 2-0	Mar	5	A Wrexham	W 2-0
Oct	2	A Doncaster	W 1-0			12 H Barrow	L 0-1
	4	A Bradford PA	D 1-1			19 A Hartlepools	W 2-0
	9	H Port Vale	W 1-0			26 H Doncaster R	D 0-0
	16	A Halifax	W 2-0	Apr	2	A Lincoln C	D 1-1
	20	H Barnsley	W 3-0			8 A Crewe A	L 1-2
	23	H Chester	W 1-0			9 H Colchester	L 0-1
	30	A Notts Co	D 1-1			11 H Crewe A	W 2-1
Nov	6	H Lincoln C	W 4-1			15 A Stockport	L 0-1
	20	H Stockport	L 1-4			23 H Tranmere R	W 2-1
	23	H Bradford PA	W 2-1			25 A Southport	D 3-3
	26	A Tranmere Rov	W 1-0			30 A Colchester	W 2-0
Dec	11	A Barnsley	L 0-1	May	2	H Halifax	W 1-0
	27	H Aldershot	W 5-1			9 H Notts Co	W 2-0
Jan	1	A Port Vale	D 0-0			21 A Darlington	D 0-0

Division Four Table in 1965/6

	P	W	D	L	F	A	Pts
Doncaster R	46	24	11	11	85	54	59
Darlington	46	25	9	12	72	53	59
Torquay	46	24	10	12	72	49	58
Colchester	46	23	10	13	70	47	56
Tranmere R	46	24	8	14	93	66	56
Luton T	46	24	8	14	90	70	56
Chester	46	20	12	14	79	70	52
Notts Co	46	19	12	15	61	53	50
Newport Co	46	18	12	16	75	75	48
Southport	46	18	12	16	68	69	48
Bradford PA	46	21	5	20	102	92	47
Barrow	46	16	15	15	72	76	47
Stockport Co	46	18	6	22	71	70	42
Crewe A	46	16	9	21	61	63	41
Halifax T	46	15	11	20	67	75	41
Barnsley	46	15	10	21	74	78	40
Aldershot	46	15	10	21	75	84	40
Hartlepools	46	16	8	22	63	75	40
Port Vale	46	15	9	22	48	59	39
Chesterfield	46	13	13	20	62	78	39
Rochdale	46	16	5	25	71	87	37
Lincoln C	46	13	11	22	57	82	37
Bradford C	46	12	13	21	63	94	37
Wrexham	46	13	9	24	72	104	35

United's League Record in 1971/2
(when they were last relegated to Division Four)

Aug	14	H Chesterfield	W 3-2		Jan	1	H Swansea C	L	1-4
	21	A Shrewsbury	L 0-2			8	A Bristol Rov	L	0-2
	28	H Bristol Rov	D 1-1			22	A Oldham Ath	L	0-1
Sep	1	H Bradford C	W 2-1			29	H York City	L	0-1
	4	A Rotherham	D 2-2		Feb	12	H Tranmere R	L	0-1
	11	H Walsall	D 2-2			19	A Barnsley	D	0-0
	13	H Rochdale	D 1-1			26	H Bournemouth	L	0-2
	18	A Swansea C	D 0-0		Mar	4	A Blackburn R	L	0-1
	25	H Brighton	D 2-2			11	A Wrexham	W	2-1
	29	H Oldham Ath	L 0-2			14	A Halifax T	D	0-0
Oct	2	A Rochdale	L 0-5			18	H Shrewsbury	W	2-0
	9	H Wrexham	L 2-3		Mar	22	H Halifax T	W	2-0
	16	A Chesterfield	L 0-2			25	A Walsall	L	0-1
	18	A York City	L 1-3			31	A Brighton	L	1-3
	22	A Tranmere R	L 0-2		Apr	1	H Plymouth A	W	2-1
	30	H Barnsley	L 1-2			8	H Notts Co	D	1-1
Nov	6	A Bournemouth	L 0-1			12	H Aston Villa	W	2-1
	13	H Blackburn R	W 3-1			15	A Port Vale	D	0-0
	27	H Port Vale	W 3-0			19	A Bolton W	L	0-2
Dec	4	A Mansfield T	D 0-0			22	H Mansfield	L	0-1
	18	H Rotherham	L 0-1			26	A Bradford C	W	1-0
	27	A Plymouth A	L 1-3			29	A Aston Villa	L	1-5
					May	3	A Notts Co	L	1-2
						5	H Bolton W	D	1-1

Division Three Table in 1971/2

	P	W	D	L	F	A	Pts
Aston Villa	46	32	6	8	85	32	70
Brighton	46	27	11	8	82	47	65
Bournemouth	46	23	16	7	73	37	62
Notts Co	46	25	12	9	74	44	62
Rotherham	46	20	15	11	69	52	55
Bristol R	46	21	12	13	75	56	54
Bolton W	46	17	16	13	51	41	50
Plymouth A	46	20	10	16	74	64	50
Walsall	46	15	18	13	62	57	48
Blackburn R	46	19	9	18	54	57	47
Oldham Ath	46	17	11	18	59	63	45
Shrewsbury	46	17	10	19	73	65	44
Chesterfield	46	18	8	20	57	57	44
Swansea C	46	17	10	19	46	59	44
Port Vale	46	13	15	18	43	59	41
Wrexham	46	16	8	22	59	63	40
Halifax T	46	13	12	21	48	61	38
Rochdale	46	12	13	21	57	83	37
York City	46	12	12	22	57	66	36
Tranmere R	46	10	16	20	50	71	36
Mansfield	46	8	20	18	41	63	36
Barnsley	46	9	18	19	32	64	36
Torquay	46	10	12	24	41	69	32
Bradford C	46	11	10	25	45	77	32

United's League Record in 1984/5

(when they successfully sought Re-election after Finishing Bottom
for the first time since their inaugural year in the Football League)

Aug	25	A Crewe A	L	0-3	
Sep	1	H Stockport	D	0-0	
	8	A Swindon T	W	3-1	
	15	H Port Vale	L	1-3	
	18	H Darlington	D	1-1	
	22	A Rochdale	D	0-0	
	29	H Peterboro	D	0-0	
Oct	2	A Colchester	L	1-2	
	6	H Wrexham	W	4-3	
	13	A Mansfield	L	0-1	
	20	H Hartlepool	L	0-1	
	23	A Scunthorpe	L	0-2	
	27	A Tranmere	L	1-3	
Nov	3	H Hereford	W	1-0	
	6	H Halifax	D	1-1	
	10	A Chester	W	1-0	
	24	H Chesterfield	L	0-1	
Dec	1	A Bury	L	1-3	
	15	H Blackpool	L	0-2	
	22	H Southend	D	2-2	
	26	A Exeter	L	3-4	
	29	A Northampton	L	1-3	
Jan	1	H Aldershot	L	1-3	

	5	H Crewe A	D	0-0
	26	A Port Vale	D	2-2
Feb	2	A Peterboro	L	0-1
	9	H Rochdale	W	1-0
	23	A Hereford	L	0-1
	26	H Swindon T	D	0-0
Mar	2	H Tranmere	D	1-1
	5	H Scunthorpe	D	0-0
	9	A Hartlepool	L	1-3
Mar	19	H Mansfield T	W	1-0
	23	A Wrexham	L	0-2
	30	A Halifax	W	1-0
Apr	1	A Stockport Co	W	2-1
	6	H Exeter C	D	1-1
	9	A Aldershot	L	0-1
	13	H Chester C	W	2-0
	16	H Colchester	D	1-1
	20	A Chesterfield	L	0-1
	27	H Bury	L	0-2
May	4	A Blackpool	D	3-3
	6	H Northampton	L	0-2
	11	A Southend	L	0-1
	14	A Darlington	L	0-1

Division Four Table in 1984/5

	P	W	D	L	F	A	Pts
Chesterfield	46	26	13	7	64	35	91
Blackpool	46	24	14	8	73	39	86
Darlington	46	24	13	9	66	49	85
Bury	46	24	12	10	76	50	84
Hereford	46	22	11	13	65	47	77
Tranmere R	46	24	3	19	83	66	75
Colchester	46	20	14	12	87	65	74
Swindon T	46	21	9	16	62	58	72
Scunthorpe	46	19	14	13	83	62	71
Crewe A	46	18	12	16	65	69	66
Peterborough	46	16	14	16	54	53	62
Port Vale	46	14	18	14	61	59	60
Aldershot	46	17	8	21	56	63	59
Mansfield T	46	13	18	15	41	38	57
Wrexham	46	15	9	22	67	70	54
Chester	46	15	9	22	60	72	54
Rochdale	46	13	14	19	55	69	53
Exeter C	46	13	14	19	57	79	53
Hartlepool	46	14	10	22	54	67	52
Southend	46	13	11	22	58	83	50
Halifax T	46	15	5	26	42	69	50
Stockport Co	46	13	8	25	58	79	47
Northampton T	46	14	5	27	53	74	47
Torquay U	46	9	14	23	38	63	41

United's League Record in 1985/6
(when they finished bottom of the League for the Second Year Running)

Aug	17	A Scunthorpe	L	0-4
	24	H Rochdale	L	1-2
	26	A Swindon T	L	1-2
	31	H Colchester	W	2-1
Sep	7	A Preston NE	L	0-4
	14	H Chester C	L	0-3
	18	A Peterborough	L	0-2
	21	H Hartlepool	L	1-3
	28	A Crewe A	L	0-1
Oct	1	H Halifax	W	2-0
	5	H Stockport	W	4-3
	12	A Hereford	L	1-4
	19	H Northampton	D	1-1
	22	A Burnley	L	0-3
	26	A Mansfield	L	0-4
Nov	2	H Orient	D	2-2
	6	H Southend	D	2-2
	9	A Tranmere R	L	0-2
	23	H Wrexham	L	1-3
Dec	14	H Cambridge	D	1-1
	17	A Port Vale	L	0-1
	21	A Rochdale	L	0-5
	28	H Swindon T	L	0-1

Jan	11	A Colchester	D	0-0
	18	H Scunthorpe	W	1-0
	25	A Chester C	L	1-3
Feb	1	H Preston NE	W	1-0
	4	H Burnley	W	2-0
Mar	1	H Crewe A	D	0-0
	7	A Stockport Co	D	1-1
	11	H Peterborough	W	2-0
	15	H Hereford	W	2-1
Mar	18	A Orient	L	2-4
	22	H Mansfield	L	1-2
	26	A Exeter C	D	2-2
	29	A Aldershot	D	1-1
Apr	1	H Exeter C	L	1-2
	4	A Southend	W	2-1
	8	H Aldershot	L	1-2
	12	H Tranmere R	L	1-2
	14	A Halifax T	D	0-0
	15	A Hartlepool	L	0-1
	19	A Wrexham	L	2-3
	26	H Port Vale	L	0-1
	29	A Northampton	L	1-5
May	3	A Cambridge	L	0-3

Division Four Table in 1985/6

	P	W	D	L	F	A	Pts
Swindon T	46	32	6	8	82	43	102
Chester C	46	23	15	8	83	50	84
Mansfield T	46	23	12	11	74	47	81
Port Vale	46	21	16	9	67	37	79
Orient	46	20	12	14	79	64	72
Colchester	46	19	13	14	88	63	70
Hartlepool	46	20	10	16	68	67	70
Northampton	46	18	10	18	79	58	64
Southend	46	18	10	18	69	67	64
Hereford	46	18	10	18	74	73	64
Stockport Co	46	17	13	16	63	71	64
Crewe A	46	18	9	19	54	61	63
Wrexham	46	17	9	20	68	80	60
Burnley	46	16	11	19	60	65	59
Scunthorpe	46	15	14	17	50	55	59
Aldershot	46	17	7	22	66	74	58
Peterborough	46	13	17	16	52	64	56
Rochdale	46	14	13	19	57	77	55
Tranmere R	46	15	9	22	74	73	54
Halifax	46	14	12	20	60	71	54
Exeter C	46	13	15	18	47	59	54
Cambridge	46	15	9	22	65	80	54
Preston NE	46	11	10	25	54	89	43
Torquay U	46	9	10	27	43	88	37

United's League Fixtures in 1986/7
(when they pulled off the "Great Escape")

Aug	23	H Burnley	D	1-1
	31	A Northampton	L	0-1
Sep	6	H Wrexham	W	2-1
	12	A Colchester	L	0-3
	16	A Cambridge	D	3-3
	20	H Aldershot	D	2-2
	27	A Preston NE	D	1-1
	30	H Stockport	D	0-0
Oct	3	A Tranmere	D	2-2
	11	H Halifax T	W	1-0
	17	A Scunthorpe	L	0-2
	21	H Lincoln C	L	0-1
	25	H Swansea C	L	3-5
	31	A Southend U	L	0-4
Nov	4	A Hartlepool	L	1-2
	8	H Wolves	L	1-2
	22	H Hereford U	D	1-1
	29	A Rochdale	D	3-3
Dec	13	A Crewe A	L	0-1
	26	A Exeter C	D	2-2
	27	H Orient	D	2-2
Jan	3	A Hereford U	D	2-2
	24	A Wrexham	L	1-2

	31	H Colchester	W	3-1
Feb	7	H Cambridge U	W	1-0
	14	A Aldershot	D	1-1
	21	H Preston NE	L	0-2
	24	H Northampton	L	0-1
	27	A Stockport	D	0-0
Mar	3	H Southend U	W	2-1
	14	H Scunthorpe	D	2-2
	17	A Lincoln C	D	1-1
	21	A Halifax T	W	4-2
	28	H Tranmere R	L	0-2
Mar	31	H Peterborough	W	1-0
Apr	4	A Wolves	L	0-1
	7	A Swansea C	W	I-0
	11	H Hartlepool	L	0-1
	14	A Burnley	D	2-2
	18	A Cardiff C	L	1-3
	20	H Exeter C	D	1-1
	25	A Peterborough	L	1-2
	28	H Cardiff C	W	1-0
May	2	H Rochdale	W	2-1
	4	A Orient	L	2-3
	9	H Crewe A	D	2-2

Division Four Table in 1986/7

	P	W	D	L	F	A	Pts
Northampton T	46	30	9	7	103	53	99
Preston NE	46	26	12	8	72	47	90
Southend U	46	25	5	16	68	55	80
Wolves	46	24	7	15	69	50	79
Colchester U	46	21	7	18	64	56	70
Aldershot	46	21	10	16	64	57	70
Orient	46	20	9	17	64	61	69
Scunthorpe U	46	18	12	16	73	57	66
Wrexham	46	15	20	11	70	51	65
Peterborough	46	17	14	15	57	50	65
Cambridge U	46	17	11	18	60	62	62
Swansea C	46	17	11	18	56	61	62
Cardiff C	46	15	16	15	48	50	61
Exeter C	46	11	23	12	53	49	56
Halifax T	46	15	10	21	59	74	55
Hereford U	46	14	11	21	60	61	53
Crewe A	46	13	14	19	70	72	53
Hartlepool	46	11	18	17	44	65	51
Stockport Co	46	13	12	21	40	71	51
Tranmere R	46	11	17	18	54	72	50
Rochdale	46	11	17	18	54	73	50
Burnley	46	12	13	21	53	74	49
Torquay U	46	10	18	18	56	72	48
Lincoln C	46	12	12	22	45	65	48

United's FA Cup Record since joining the League in 1927

Season	Rd	H/A	Opponent	Result		Season	Rd	H/A	Opponent	Result
1927/28			Did not enter			1953/54	1	H	Bristol C	L 1-3
1928/29	1	A	Gillingham	D 0-0		1954/55	1	H	Cambridge	W 4-0
	R	H	Gillingham	W 5-1			2	A	Blyth Spartans	W 3-1
	2	H	Exeter C	L 0-1			3	A	Leeds U	D 2-2
1929/30	1	A	Bournemouth	L 0-2			R	H	Leeds U	W 4-0
1930/31	1	A	Southend U	W 1-0			4	H	Huddersfield	L 0-1
	2	A	Accrington St	W 1-0		1955/56	1	H	Colchester	W 2-0
	3	A	Bury	D 1-1			2	A	Shrewsbury	D 0-0
	R	H	Bury	L 1-2 *			R	H	Shrewsbury	W 5-1
1931/32	1	H	Southend U	L 1-3			3	H	Birmingham	L 1-7
1932/33	1	H	Bournemouth	D 0-0		1956/57	1	A	Ely City	W 6-2
	R	A	Bournemouth	D 2-2 *			2	H	Plymouth A	W 1-0
	R	N	Bournemouth	W 3-2			3	A	New Brighton	L 1-2
	2	H	QPR	D 1-1		1957/58	1	A	Peterborough	D 3-3
	R	A	QPR	L 1-3			R	H	Peterborough	W 1-0
1933/34	1	H	Margate	D 1-1			2	H	Southend U	D 1-1
	R	A	Margate	W 2-0			R	A	Southend U	L 1-2
	2	A	Northampton	L 0-3		1958/59	1	H	Port Vale	W 1-0
1934/35	1	A	Dulwich Hamlet	W 2-1			2	H	Watford	W 2-0
	2	A	Wigan Ath	L 2-3			3	A	Newport Co	D 0-0
1935/36	1	A	Dulwich Hamlet	W 3-2			R	H	Newport Co	L 0-1
	2	A	Notts Co	L 0-3		1959/60	1	H	Northampton	W 7-1
1936/37	1	A	Clapton Orient	L 1-2			2	A	Gillingham	D 2-2
1937/38	1	H	Clapton Orient	L 1-2			R	H	Gillingham	L 1-2
1938/39	1	H	Exeter C	W 3-1		1960/61	1	A	Weymouth	W 3-1
	2	A	Ipswich T	L 1-4			2	H	Peterborough	L 1-3
1939/45			Suspended due to war			1961/62	1	H	Harwich	W 5-1
1945/46	1	H	Newport Co	L 0-1			2	H	Peterborough	L 1-4
2nd leg	1	A	Newport Co	D 1-1		1962/63	1	A	Northampton	W 2-1
1946/47	1	A	Ipswich T	L 0-2			2	A	Shrewsbury	L 1-2
1947/48	1	A	Watford	D 1-1		1963/64	1	H	Barnet	W 6-2
	R	H	Watford	W 3-0			2	H	Aldershot	L 2-3
	2	A	Northampton	D 1-1		1964/65	1	A	Canterbury C	W 6-0
	R	H	Northampton	W 2-0			2	H	Colchester	W 2-0
	3	A	Stockport Co	L 0-3			3	H	Spurs	D 3-3
1948/49	1	A	Peterborough	W 1-0			R	A	Spurs	L 1-5
	2	H	Norwich C	W 3-1		1965/66	1	A	Shrewsbury	L 1-2
	3	H	Coventry C	W 1-0		1966/67	1	A	Aldershot	L 1-2
	4	A	Brentford	L 0-1		1967/68	1	H	Colchester	D 1-1
1949/50	1	A	Gravesend	W 3-1			R	A	Colchester	L 1-2
	2	A	Northampton	L 2-4		1968/69	1	A	Hereford U	D 0-0
1950/51	1	A	Nottm Forest	L 1-6			R	H	Hereford U	W 4-2
1951/52	1	H	Bromley	W 3-2			2	A	Reading	D 0-0
	2	A	Swindon T	D 3-3			R	H	Reading	L 1-2
	R	H	Swindon T	D 1-1 *						
	R	N	Swindon T	L 1-3						
1952/53	1	A	Peterborough	L 1-2						

92

Season	Rnd	H/A	Opponent	Result	Score		Season	Rnd	H/A	Opponent	Result	Score
1969/70	1	A	Tamworth	L	1-2		1988/89	1	H	Fareham Town	D	2-2
1970/71	1	H	Aston Villa	W	3-1			R	A	Fareham Town	W	3-2
	2	A	Chelmsford C	W	1-0			2	A	Yeovil Town	D	1-1
	3	H	Lincoln C	W	4-3			R	H	Yeovil Town	W	1-0
	4	A	Leicester C	L	0-3			3	A	Sheffield Wed	L	1-5
1971/72	1	H	Nuneaton Bo	W	1-0		1989/90	1	A	Sutton U	D	1-1
	2	A	Barnet	W	4-1			R	H	Sutton U	W	4-0
	3	A	Bolton W	L	1-2			2	A	Basingstoke	W	3-2
1972/73	1	H	Hereford U	W	3-0			3	H	West Ham Utd	W	1-0
	2	H	Newport Co	L	0-1			4	A	Blackpool	L	0-1
1973/74	1	A	Hereford U	L	1-3							
1974/75	1	H	Northampton	L	0-1							
1975/76	1	A	Hereford U	L	0-2							
1976/77	1	H	Hillingdon B	L	1-2							
1977/78	1	H	Southend U	L	1-2							
1978/79	1	A	Walsall	W	2-0							
	2	A	AP Leamington	W	1-0							
	3	A	Newcastle U	L	1-3							
1979/80	1	A	Gravesend	W	1-0							
	2	H	Swindon T	D	3-3							
	R	A	Swindon T	L	2-3							
1980/81	1	H	Barton Rov	W	2-0							
	2	A	St Albans C	D	1-1							
	R	H	St Albans C	W	4-1							
	3	A	Barnsley	L	1-2							
1981/82	1	A	Bristol C	D	0-0							
	R	H	Bristol C	L	1-2							
1982/83	1	A	Colchester U	W	2-0							
	2	H	Carshalton	W	4-1							
	3	A	Oxford U	D	1-1							
	R	H	Oxford U	W	2-1							
	4	H	Sheffield Wed	L	2-3							
1983/84	1	H	Colchester U	L	1-2							
1984/85	1	H	Yeovil T	W	2-0							
	2	A	Orient	L	0-3							
1985/86	1	A	Windsor & Eton	D	1-1							
	R	H	Windsor & Eton	W	3-0							
	2	A	Newport Co	D	1-1							
	R	H	Newport Co	L	2-3 *							
1986/87	1	A	Aldershot	L	0-1							
1987/88	1	A	Bognor Regis T	W	3-0							
	2	A	Bristol City	W	1-0							
	3	A	Coventry City	L	0-2							

*After extra time

United's Year by Year League Cup Record

Season	Rd	H/A	Opponent	Result	Score
1960/61	1		Bye		
	2	H	Plymouth A	D	1-1
	R	A	Plymouth A	L	1-2
1961/62	1	A	Bournemouth	D	2-2
	R	H	Bournemouth	L	0-1
1962/63	1	H	Oxford U	W	2-0
	2	H	Carlisle U	L	1-2
1963/64	1	H	Brighton	L	1-2
1964/65	1	A	Colchester U	D	1-1
	R	H	Colchester U	W	3-0
	2	H	Notts Co	L	1-2
1965/66	1	A	Shrewsbury T	L	0-3
1966/67	1	A	Exeter City	D	2-2
	R	H	Exeter City	L	1-2
1967/68	1	H	Exeter City	D	0-0
	R	A	Exeter City	W	3-0
	2	A	Gillingham	D	2-2
	R	H	Gillingham	W	2-0
	3	A	Lincoln City	L	2-4
1968/69	1	A	Swindon Town	L	1-2
1969/70	1	A	Plymouth A	D	2-2
	R	H	Plymouth A	W	1-0
	2	A	Tranmere Rov	L	1-2
1970/71	1	H	Bournemouth	D	1-1
	R	A	Bournemouth	W	2-1
	2	H	Preston NE	L	1-3
1971/72	1	A	Newport Co	W	2-1
	2	H	Oldham Ath	W	2-1
	3	H	Spurs	L	1-4
1972/73	1	H	Portsmouth	L	1-2
1973/74	1	H	Plymouth A	L	0-2
1974/75	1	A	Newport Co	L	0-1
1975/76	1	A	Swansea City	1	2-1
2nd leg	1	H	Swansea City	W	5-3
	2	H	Exeter City	D	1-1
	R	A	Exeter City	W	2-1
	3	H	Doncaster R	D	1-1
	R	A	Doncaster R	L	0-3
1976/77	1	A	Bournemouth	D	0-0
2nd leg	1	H	Bournemouth	W	1-0
	2	H	Burnley	W	1-0
	3	H	Swansea City	L	1-2
1977/78	1	H	Cardiff City	W	1-0
2nd leg	1	A	Cardiff City	L	2-3
	R	A	Cardiff City	L	1-2
1978/79	1	A	Plymouth A	D	1-1
2nd leg	1	H	Plymouth A	L	1-2
1979/80	1	H	Bristol Rov	L	1-2
2nd leg	1	A	Bristol Rov	W	3-1 *
	2	A	Notts Co	D	0-0
2nd leg	2	H	Notts Co	L	0-1
1980/81	1	H	Cardiff City	D	0-0
2nd leg	1	A	Cardiff City	L	1-2
1981/82	1	H	Newport Co	L	2-3
2nd leg	1	A	Newport Co	D	0-0
1982/83	1	A	Bristol Rov	D	2-2
2nd leg	1	H	Bristol Rov	L	0-4
1983/84	1	A	Newport Co	W	3-2
2nd leg	1	H	Newport Co	W	1-0
	2	H	Manchester C	D	0-0
2nd leg	2	A	Manchester C	L	0-6
1984/85	1	A	Plymouth A	L	0-1
2nd leg	1	H	Plymouth A	L	0-1
1985/86	1	H	Swindon Town	L	1-2
2nd leg	1	A	Swindon Town	D	2-2
1986/87	1	A	Swindon Town	L	0-3
2nd leg	1	H	Swindon Town	L	2-3
1987/88	1	H	Swansea City	W	2-1
2nd leg	1	A	Swansea City	D	1-1
	2	H	Spurs	W	1-0
2nd leg	2	A	Spurs	L	0-3
1988/89	1	H	Reading	L	0-1
2nd leg	1	A	Reading	L	1-3
1989/90	1	H	Hereford	L	0-1
2nd leg	1	A	Hereford	L	0-3

*After extra time

94

Year by Year Record of United's Highest Scorers in the League since they joined in 1927/8

1927/28	Herbert Turner	11	1962/63	Brian Handley	20
1928/29	Cyril Hemingway	11	1963/64	Robin Stubbs	24
1929/30	Joe Pointon	18	1964/65	Robin Stubbs	31
1930/31	Jimmy Trotter	25	1965/66	Tommy Spratt	18
1931/32	Bill Clayson	14	1966/67	Robin Stubbs	21
1932/33	George Stabb	24	1967/68	Robin Stubbs	9
1933/34	George Stabb	13	1968/69	Robin Stubbs	18
1934/35	Albert Hutchinson	19	1969/70	Alan Welsh	15
1935/36	Albert Hutchinson	10	1970/71	John Rudge	17
1936/37	Ben Morton	23	1971/72	Alan Welsh	10
1937/38	Ben Morton	10	1972/73	Mike Trebilcock	10
1938/39	Ralph Allen	15	1973/74	Eddie Rowles	10
1946/47	Jack Conley	23	1974/75	Cliff Myers	8
1947/48	Ron Shaw	17	1975/76	Willie Brown	14
1948/49	Jack Conley	19	1976/77	Willie Brown	18
1949/50	Jack Conley	14	1977/78	Willie Brown	12
1950/51	Sammy Collins	11	1978/79	Les Lawrence	17
1951/52	Sammy Collins	22	1979/80	Steve Cooper	17
1952/53	Sammy Collins	27	1980/81	Gerry Fell	12
1953/54	Sammy Collins	17	1981/82	Tony Brown	11
1954/55	Sammy Collins	26	1982/83	Steve Cooper	15
1955/56	Sammy Collins	40	1983/84	Colin Barnes	8
1956/57	Sammy Collins	30	1984/85	Mario Walsh	5
1957/58	Tommy Northcott	13	1985/86	Steve Phillips	8
1958/59	Tommy Northcott	20	1986/87	Paul Dobson	16
1959/60	Graham Bond	21	1987/88	Paul Dobson	22
1960/61	Tommy Northcott	25	1988/89	Dean Edwards	8
1961/62	Ernie Pym	19	1989/90	Mark Loram	12

Managers since 1946:

Billy Butler, Jack Butler, John McNeil, Bob John, Alex Massie, Eric Webber, Frank O'Farrell, Allan Brown, Jack Edwards, Malcolm Musgrove, Frank O'Farrell, Mike Green, Frank O'Farrell, Bruce Rioch, David Webb, John Sims, Stuart Morgan, Cyril Knowles, Dave Smith.

Honours:

Champions Southern League 1926/27
Football League best - Runners Up Division Three (South) 1956/57
3rd in Division Four (promoted) 1959/60
3rd in Division Four (promoted) 1965/66
Division Three highest position – 4th in 1967/68
FA Cup – Reached 4th round 1948/49, 1954/55, 1970/71, 1982/83, 1989/90.
Never reached the 5th round
League Cup – never past the 3rd round
Sherpa Van Trophy Runners Up 1988/89

Record Victory:

9-0 v. Swindon Town in Division Three (South) 8 March 1952

Record Defeat:

2-10 v. Fulham in Division Three (South) 7 September 1931, and v. Luton Town in Division Three (South) 2 September 1933

Most League Points:

For 2 points for a win – 60 in Division Four, 1959/60
For 3 points for a win – 77 in Division Four 1987/88

Most League Goals:

89 in Division Three (South) 1956/57

Highest Scorer:

Sammy Collins – 40 in Division Three (South) 1955/56

Highest Scorer In Total :

Sammy Collins – 204 league goals between 1948 and 1958

Most league games:

Dennis Lewis – 443 – between 1947 and 1959

Record Fee Paid:

£60,000 for Wes Saunders from Dundee, 1990

Record Fee Received:

£180,000 from Manchester United for Lee Sharpe, May 1988

Torquay United's Record with Exeter City and Plymouth Argyle in their league meetings since 1958/9:

	P	W	L	D	F	A
Exeter	30	4	12	14	33	51
Plymouth	8	4	0	4	10	16